the tin violin

The adventures of Joseph Emidy

A true Cornish tale

Alan M. Kent

---

the tin violin

The adventures of Joseph Emidy
A true Cornish tale

First published by Francis Boutle Publishers
272 Alexandra Park Road
London N22 7BG
Tel/Fax: +44 (0)20 8889 7744
Email: info@francisboutle.co.uk
www.francisboutle.co.uk

ISBN 978 1 903427 42 2

Praise for BishBashBosh Productions

"One of the most innovative theatre companies in Britain, a crucible of creativity that rivals anything in the West End… Last year's *Surfing Tommies* was a cracker." *Sunday Times*

"Pick of the week: *Surfing Tommies*… Alan M. Kent's award-winning drama." *Guardian*

"A giant of a performance... Make sure you don't miss it this time around." *Western Morning News*

"As exciting as the play is on the printed page, it is electrifying in performance… The cast perform handsomely and are as compelling as they are courageous." *The Cornishman*

"Thorough, meticulous and thought-provoking." *Morning Star*

"Nolan was hugely entertaining and touching… A spirited and engaging Molly Weaver bestrode both past and present." *The Stage*

"The company balance the sorrow with humour and even integrated an element of audience participation." *Yorkshire Evening Post*

"I have only praise for Kent's writing. He has an amazing ability to use Cornish history deep-rooted within the characters and their lives and then combine it with the sort of comedy that has you roaring with laughter." *Cornwall Today*

"*Surfing Tommies*' gobbets of humorous scenes are acted with glee by the small and accomplished cast…" *What's on Stage*

BishBashBosh Productions

BishBashBosh Productions are a production company from Cornwall dedicated to commissioning, developing and producing theatre, film and media – new work that offers a response to Cornish issues, trends and events. We find our inspiration in landscape, community, multiculturalism, Celticity, and literature and theatre across frontiers. In this way we hope to develop a national theatre for Cornwall (*Gwaryjy Kenedhlek rag Kernow*).

Since 2007 we have produced critically-acclaimed productions in Cornwall and across the United Kingdom, including *Oogly es Sin*, *Surfing Tommies* and *A Mere Interlude*. We aim to develop new work through events, collaborations, workshops, readings, research and literary programmes. Our remit is also within education, to work with students and teachers in and outside of Cornwall.

This tour of *The Tin Violin* was partly funding by Feast (Community Artist Funding in Cornwall), the Arts Council England and the generous sponsors of BishBashBosh Productions.

For BishBashBosh Productions:

Patron	Benjamin Luxon CBE
Artistic Directors	Dean Nolan and Alan M. Kent
Associate Directors	John Hoggarth and Ria Parry
Associate Artists	Trevor Cuthbertson, Mbuguah Goro, Jamie Trotter, Joanne Clare, Molly Weaver, Ed Williams, Sally Crooks, Holly Kavanagh, Toby Nicholas, Stephen Robinson, Simon Harvey, Oraine Johnson, Steve Jacobs, Alex Kristoffy and Robin Kristoffy
Maker	Mike Banks
Music	The People's String Foundation (Ben Sutcliffe and Zaid Al-Rabiki)
Choreography	Cscape: Dance Company (Sally Williams and Helen Tiplady)
Education	Caroline Swain
Advertising	Lianne Crocker
Press Officer	Jane Verity
Publisher	Francis Boutle Publishers

info@bishbashboshproductions.co.uk
www.bishbashboshproductions.co.uk

The first professional production of *The Tin Violin* was given in June 2008 with the following performers:

Actor 1: Mbuguah Goro
Actor 2: Trevor Cuthbertson
Acrot 3: Joanne Clare

Directed by John Hoggarth
Produced by Dean Nolan for BishBashBosh Productions
Stage Management by Victoria Guy

* * * *

The 2012 production of *The Tin Violin* opened in May 2012 at the Minack Theatre Cornwall, with the following performers:

Actor 1: Oraine Johnson
Actor 2: Steve Jacobs
Acrot 3: Molly Weaver

Chorus: Alex Kristoffy and Robin Kristoffy
Dancers: Sally Williams, Helen Tiplady,

Directed by Dean Nolan and John Hoggarth
Produced by Dean Nolan for BishBashBosh Productions
Stage Management by Stephen Robinson

Acknowledgements

I am indebted to the researches of Richard McGrady on the world of Josh Emidy, and to Brycchan Carey on Cornwall and the slave trade in the eighteenth century. Thanks also to Lee Mixashawn Rosie, the fourth great-grandson or Josh Emidy and the many other Emidy relatives who have contracted me since the play's first run. I would like to thank Capoeira Gear UK and my continued thanks to the Royal Institution of Cornwall, and to BBC Radio Cornwall for realising the possibilities of my dramas for radio and for publicising them on air.

Audience members who have been following the work of the company will note that this is a 're-stringed' version of *The Tin Violin*. When the show first toured in 2008, it was not possible to complete all that the script then demanded. This new version comes with an extended Act 3, Scene 3 and some extra moments of action.

Alan M. Kent
Lanbrebois/Probus
May 2012

Our Sponsors for 2012

BishBashBosh Productions would like to thank all our corporate sponsors for supporting the 2012 Britain-wide tour of *The Tin Violin*:

Atlantic Cottage Holidays
Beyond Organic Skincare Ltd
Bunters
Carn Glaze Caverns
Driftwood Spars
Hawkins Arms, Probus
Healthy Boxes
Jo Jingles Ltd
Loenter
Mobius Kite School
Pasty Line
Roskilly's Ltd
Tiers of Temptation
Tree Inn, Stratton
University College Falmouth
Arts Council England
Bodmin and Wenford Railway
Campers in Cornwall
Coach House Cottages
Feast
Hawkins Motors
Jane Adams Ceramics
Len Nolan
Mark Jennings Violin Maker
Newquay Zoo
Perranporth Surf School
Skinners Brewery
Treasure Park, Tolgus Mill
Truro and Penwith College

We would also like to thank the following BishBashBosh buddies for their continuing support:

J. Utteridge, M. Crome, E. Wooderson, Ruth Stock, G.Clarke, M. Roskrow, Pat Owen, Trevor Gardner, Peter Pullen, Gail Ward, Tony McLennan, Zoe Hughes, Steve Endean, Wendy Woodcock, Tom Kennedy, Jimmy Carveth, Jamie Caruana, Robert Holland, Matthew Dearing, Mark and Jane Champion, Colin and Sylvia Honey, Gary Collins, Julia Dunstan, Gary Baker, Rhia Rogers and Derek Wills.

If you would like to become a BishBashBosh buddy please contact:
dean@bishbashboshproductions.co.uk

FEAST harnesses the many talents and energies of Cornwall's artists and communities to create inspiring opportunities for people to come together and enjoy high quality arts as participants and audiences.

FEAST brings artists together with community volunteers to launch or invigorate local festivals and events. We also work with partner orgaisations to offer new creative ways of tackling some of the social, economic or environmental issues facing Cornwall.

We invite you to get involved as an artist, a community producer or participant. To find out how click on www.feastcornwall.org

For more information visit www.feastcornwall.org

Opposite page. Top: Catherine Self (Baptista Trewethen) and Holly Kavanagh (Ellen Hambly) from the 2010 production of *A Mere Interlude*. Below: Mbuguah Goro (Joseph Emidy) from the 2008 prodcution of *The Tin Violin*.

This page: Dean Nolan as Anthony Payne, the Cornish Giant in *Ooogly Es Sin*

Top: Dean Nolan (Jimmy 'Dunkey' Tamblyn), Ed Williams (Robert Walling) and Trevor Cuthbertson (Cap'n William Tresawna). Bottom: Dean Nolan and Trevor Cuthbertson from *Surfing Tommies*, 2009

Rehearsals for *The Tin Violin*, 2012. Top: Alex Kristoffy, Robin Kristoffy, Oraine Johnson with director Dean Nolan. Bottom: Molly Weaver with Robin and Alex Kristoffy

Biographies

Oraine Johnson – *Josh Emidy*

Oraine Johnson is an actor, singer and dancer. He studied at the Birmingham Theatre school for three years and went on to graduate with a BA in acting at Leeds Metropolitan university. Oraine has performed in theatres nationwide, including as Crooks in *Of Mice & Men*, the Reverend Hale in *The Crucible*, and recently in a two man show *Rivers To Cross* with Sylvester Williams (*East Enders*, *Bullet Boy*).

Steve Jacobs – *James Silk Buckingham; Eduardo Souto de Moura; Sir Edward Pellew; Jabez Pender; Zachary Hutchins*

Steve is now based in Cornwall and has worked with Wildworks, Cube, Kneehigh, Cornwall Theatre Collective and most recently with Miracle Theatre in *Tin* and *Sherlock Holmes*. He has worked at Scarborough, Ipswich and Chester Reps, The Gate, Notting Hill, Haymarket and Duke of York's theatres, and the Royal Shakespeare Company, Stratford. Other adventures include touring Brazil with Duddendance and running away with NoFitState Circus. Film & TV includes *Tin*, *The Gospel of Us* (Film version of *The Passion*), *Wycliffe*, *The Bill*, *Doc Martin*, *Wild West* and *The Vet*. Last year Steve directed *Pinocchio* with Cube Theatre, currently touring. He also worked as assistant director on the award-winning production of *The Passion*, a collaboration between Wildworks and the National Theatre of Wales.

Molly Weaver – *Maria, Queen of Portugal; Signora Grilietti; Jane Hutchins; Chorus; wardrobe*

Molly began her training at the Hub Theatre School in St Austell and went on to complete a degree in Contemporary Dance Choreography at Bath Spa University. Her first professional role was playing Mosca in *Volpone* and she went on to dance around the country, including at the opening of Jamie Oliver's restaurant Fifteen, and for the BBCs Blast projects, leading Cornwall for the BBCs Big Dance Guinness record attempt and choreographing for ITVs *Doc Martin*. Molly has toured nationally with Cscape Dance Company on their *Guilty Fingers* tour, and with Rogue Theatre Company as Lolo the Clown in *Madame Lucinda's Wonder Show*. Molly joined BishBashBosh in 2008 and she has performed in *The Tin Violin*, *Surfing Tommies* and stage managed *A Mere Interlude*. Molly has sung with several bands and now sings jazz with her act Molly the Moocha, playing Glastonbury Festival last year.

Dean Nolan – *Producer and Dirctor*

Dean was born in Cornwall and trained at the Hub Theatre School, St Austell. He spent five years with the National Youth Theatre between 1999-2004 and performed in *Nicholas Nickleby* (Lyric; Lowry, Salford), *Murder in the Cathedral* (Southwark and Westminster cathedrals), *Hanging Around* (Watch this Space – National Theatre/Kneehigh collaboration) and *The Master and Margarita* (Lyric), becoming a company manager and workshop leader. Other work includes *Riot Rebellion and Bloody Insurrection*, *Sex, Docks and Rock n Roll* and *Big Society* (with Red Ladder Theatre and Chumbawamba), *Never Say Rabbit in a Boat*, *Anyone Can Write* (Hall for Cornwall) and *Tin* (with Miracle Theatre and English Touring Opera). TV and film work includes *Ashes to Ashes* (BBC), *Weekend Retreat* (O-Region) and some commercials and short films, including the Cornish language film *Tamara*. Dean has also performed in *Oogly Es Sin*, *Surfing Tommies* and *A Mere Interlude* for BishBashBosh, where he is co-artistic director.

Alex and Robin Kristoffy – *Chorus*

Alex and Robin finished studying their A levels at Truro College last June, two of which were drama and dance. Having a year out of education before studying BAs in Drama they have pursued acting which led to the involvement in Bish Bash Bosh Productions. They have recently been accepted into the National Youth Theatre. In recent years they have performed in many amateur dramatic productions and worked as TV extras. They are really looking forward to working on their first production with Bish Bash Bosh.

Cscape – *Choreography*

Cscape Dance Company, based in Cornwall, is dedicated to producing fresh, bold and original dance theatre. For ten years they have built a strong reputation for bringing high quality dance into the heart of communities at village halls and community venues, as well as creating acclaimed site-specific work and performing on a variety of stages from Glastonbury Festival to the RSC and Trebah Gardens. Cscape have produced five touring productions – *Blonde* (2004-05), *Guilty Fingers* (2006-07), *Below* (2008), *When the Shops Shut* (2009-11) and currently *If the Shoe Fits*, a show for children. They have toured with Kneehigh Theatre in *Don John* (2008-09). The company is run by Helen Tiplady and Sally Williams who co-founded the company in 2003 with Sarah Jarvis. Performing for Cscape in the *Tin Violin*: Emily Dobson, Polly Motley, Sally Williams. Choreography: Sally Williams. Rehearsal Director: Helen Tiplady

The People's String Foundation – ***Music***

The South West is the appropriate home for the beautifully evocative, languid and lush music of The People's String Foundation. Theirs is unfamiliar territory, scaling the heights of jazz, hip-hop beat-work, Middle Eastern melodies – performed with an eye toward experimentation and nods toward the avant-garde. Essentially the brainchild of multi-instrumentalist and jazz singer Ben Sutcliffe and world/blues guitarist Zaid Al-Rikabi – the duo combine to wonderful songwriting effect but it's in their live performances that the group combine, enlisting the assistance of a troupe of inspired musicians. [The writing partnership between Sutcliffe and Al-Rikabi has been through many different phases, showcasing themselves with scoring original music for theatre, as is the case with the Bish Bash Bosh Productions, but also Rogue Theatre and some independent films.]

Stephen Robinson – ***Company Stage Manager***

Stephen joins the Bish Bash Bosh team for the second time as Company Stage Manager having worked on *Surfing Tommies*. He recently worked with Spike Theatre on their productions, *On Top of the World* and *The Olympics*, Fool's Proof Theatre's *Je Suis Dead*, Milan Govedarica's production of *Me As A Penguin* and various community arts projects with Zho Productions and Tuebrook Transnational. His passion for film has seen him join Blue Monkey Productions as an artistic producer on their recent horror film, *Leashed*, and as an actor/performer with Artemis Productions, an international street theatre company that he co-founded in 2001. Stephen lists amongst his interests, '... breaking and fixing things' a skill he hopes not to apply to the actors on this tour.

Jane Verity – ***Press officer***

Jane has five arts years PR experience, both in-house and agency. In 2010 she took the plunge and went freelance, and thoroughly enjoys the pleasures of self-employment. Press and PR Manager for Red Ladder Theatre and PR Associate for Bonner & Hindley Communications, current clients include Park Plaza Hotel Leeds, Marriott Hotel Leeds, Call Lane Social and Spawforths. Theatre clients include Trifle Gathering Productions, Dark Horse and Captain Mermaid Theatre. This is her second project with BishBashBosh, following last year's *Surfing Tommies* – one she can't wait to get started on.

Caroline Swain – ***Education officer***

Caroline graduated from Exeter University in 2011 with a degree in drama. Whilst studying Caroline also produced several plays for Exeter University Theatre Company that were performed both in Exeter and at the Edinburgh Fringe Festival. Since graduating Caroline has now returned to her roots in Cornwall to begin her career in the arts.

Lianne Crocker – ***Advertising***

Lianne has been the sponsorship manager for Bish Bash Bosh Productions for the past few years. Her aim here is to generate funds for the tour but also promote local enterprises and demonstrate the diversity and quality of businesses which are on offer within Cornwall.

She is a graduate in English Language and Literature from the Open University and also has a background in sales and marketing working for a large agency in London and abroad. In Cornwall, besides her work with the company, she works closely with Caradon Hill Area Heritage Project in East Cornwall; delivering Cornu-centric work-shops to children and adults. Her latest project runs from April to June at the Liskerett Centre where she is leading a workshop for local aspiring writers, with an aim to produce a collection of short stories set in and around East Cornwall. Lianne has also been busy writing the teaching resources for BishBasBosh Production's *The Beast of Bodmin Moor* puppet show. *The Beast* will begin touring in September.

Alan M. Kent – *Playwright*

Alan M. Kent was born in St Austell, Cornwall, and studied at the Universities of Cardiff and Exeter. He is a Lecturer in Literature for the Open University in South-West Britain, and a Visiting Lecturer in Celtic Literature at the University of La Coruña, Galicia. As well as being a prize-winning poet, novelist and dramatist, he has written extensively on Cornwall and Celtic Studies. He is the author of *The Literature of Cornwall: Continuity, Identity, Difference 1000-2000* (2000) and *Ordinalia: The Cornish Mystery Play Cycle – A Verse Translation* (2005). He has co-edited *Looking at the Mermaid: A Reader in Cornish Literature 800-1900* (2000) and *The Busy Earth: A Reader in Global Cornish Literature 1700-2000* (2008). Other prose works include *Cousin Jacks Mouth-Organ: Travels in Cornish America* (2004), *Proper Job, Charlie Curnow!* (2005), *Electric Pastyland* (2007) and *Voodoo Pilchard* (2010). Recent drama includes *Nativitas Christi* (2006), *Oogly es Sin* (2007) and *The Tin Violin* (2008) and *Surfing Tommies* (2009). His latest academic works include *The Theatre of Cornwall: Space, Place, Performance* (2009) and *Celtic Cornwall: Nation, Tradition, Invention* (2012). His collection of poetry *The Hope of Place: Selected Poems in English 1990-2000* was also published to critical acclaim in 2010 and as was his children's story *The Beast of Bodmin Moor* (2011). His latest novel, *Voog's Ocean* will be published in 2012.

A note on the characters

Actor 1 – Black male
Josh Emidy (c.1775–1835) was born in Guinea, West Africa, travelling to Brazil and Portugal before settling in Cornwall.

Actor 2 – White male
James Silk Buckingham (1786–1865), a Cornish-born journalist, author and traveller, and later, Member of Parliament for Sheffield.
Eduarado Souto De Moura (1765–1801), a Portuguese entrepreneur opening the Minas Gerais gold and diamond mines in Brazil. Died of venereal disease.
Sir Edward Pellew (1757–1833), a distinguished British Naval Commander.
Zachary Hutchins (1742–1822), born in Falmouth, a tradesman and Methodist lay preacher. The father of Jane Hutchins.

Actor 3 – White female
Maria I (1738–1816), Queen of Portugal.
Signora Griglietti (c.1775–1840), a star vocalist of Mozart's operas in Britain.
Jane Hutchins (c.1780–1840), born in Falmouth, Cornwall, the daughter of Zachary Hutchins.
Jabez Pender (1731–1801), miner, blinded by an underground explosion, the custodian of the tin violin.

Other Actors
Dancers and **Chorus**, fish jowsters of Cornwall.

Where a * comes after Chorus, this indicates that the role must be played by a performer other than Actor 3.

the tin violin

Act One

1. Guinea, West Africa.
2. The Slavers
3. Minas Gerais, Brazil
4. The Art of Capoeira
5. The Harbour at Rio de Janeiro

Act Two

1. The Teatro do Solitre, Lisbon
2. The backstreets of the city
3. The Indefatigable
4. The Battle
5. The Sighting of Kernow

Act Three

1. Falmouth Harbour
2. The Assembly Rooms, Truro
3. A Chapel Anniversary
4. The Aftermath
5. Guinea, West Africa

Act One

1. Guinea, West Africa.

Lights up. Carrying a wooden violin and bow, JAMES SILK BUCKINGHAM *steps onto stage, and speaks directly to the audience.*

JAMES: [*in ornate theatrical style*] Good day to you. My name is James Silk Buckingham. You may have heard of me. [*Pause*] I am no stranger to the ways of the world, and worked as a journalist for the 'Calcutta Journal' and founded the 'Oriential Herald and Colonial Review'. Since 1832 I have been the Member of Parliament for Sheffield. I was born though, in Flushing, Cornwall, and as a young man I began the study of music, finding it a most agreeable recommendation in female society, of which I was always fond. As I decided to be placed as speedily as possible in the way of turning this acquisition to practical account, I selected the violin as the instrument which recommends itself for its portability and convenience, as well as its charming voice.

JAMES *begins to leave the stage, while* JOSH EMIDY *enters. A transition: into Guinea, West Africa, c.1785. Lights up.* JOSH *is barefooted and wearing only traditional Guinean underclothing. He sits downstage centre, and begins softly playing a berimbau.*

JAMES: The only teacher procurable at Falmouth was an African negro, named Joseph Emidy, who was a general proficient in the art, an exquisite violinist and an excellent composer, who led at all the concerts of Cornwall, and who taught well the violin. I placed myself under his tuition for an hour's daily lesson under his own eye. In so doing, he taught me to play, and while we played together, he told me his incredible tale...

The CHORUS *enters upstage centre. All the* CHORUS *members are fish jowsters and wear hessian cloaks with hoods, white towzers (aprons), clogs and gooks (traditional head-wear) upon their heads. The* CHORUS *performs a haunting chant of words in the Cornish language, integrating with the melody of the music.*

CHORUS: Crowder… crowder… crowder…
Dean due… Dean due… Dean due…
Groudel… groudel… groudel…
Gweadar… gweadar… gweadar…
Haze gwaze… Haze gwaze… Haze gwaze…

The Cornish voices fade. JOSH *speaks gently over the melody.*

JOSH: Asalaamaalekum. Naka nga def? Numu demee? Lu bees? [*resigned*] Dara beesul.

CHORUS: Peace be with you crowder.

Pause.

JOSH: Crowder?

CHORUS: Thaas' our word fur a fiddle. How do you do? How is it? What is new? Nothing? No, something. Listen, he speaks…

Music stops. Spotlight on JOSH. *The rest of the stage is in blackness.*

JOSH: Long, long before the tin violin found me – when I was a boy – this is how I made my music: with berimbau. See my long fingers. Those fingers gained their strength here, on berimbau. Feel the wood of the bow. This string is tightly secured. In my father's tongue we called it arame. [*Pause*] See this gourd. It resonates through me. My body makes the sound you hear. With this rattle, I can accompany my playing. This stick – like a conductor's baton, yes? – is named baqueta. [*laughing*] What an orchestra! What philharmonics! See this… It is pedra. A simple pebble, just like the ones you find upon Gyllyngvase Beach…

Lights up on the CHORUS.

CHORUS: Oh yes, we d'knaw Gyllyngvase… But never mind that for now. Play for us, so we may dance… We need to dance to celebrate the world. We dance for Africa. We dance for Cornwall.

JOSH *starts to play. The* CHORUS *dances a traditional Guinean dance fused with traditional Cornish elements. After the dance, the* CHORUS *gathers around* JOSH *with interest.*

CHORUS: Josh Emidy, what was Guinea like? Tell us, for we are but simple mackerel-chewing jowster women... We want to know...

Pause.

JOSH: You ask of Guinea? Well, Guinea – the land that was my first home – was placed by graceful God's arranging between the lands of the Waalo and Sahel in the north, and the lands of the Sosso, the Songhai and the Fulani in the south. Like you, we peer upon the azure ocean. The white breakers plash against the sandy beach. Our people look to far horizons. Even though all is now distant, I still hear the names: Boké, Conakry and Faranah. Mamou, Kindia and Kankan. [*Pause*] In my mind are the stories still: the painted warriors of the empire of Ghana, heroic legends from the Battle of Kirina, the Songhai tales of creation... I still know those of Tondibi that my mother taught me. Such rhythms. Beautiful stories of my people. And I hear birds... the barbets, the hornbills, the cranes, the weavers... Everywhere was birdsong. Everywhere was music. O, 'twas like the very world sang to me.

CHORUS: A paradise then, my lover. Just like here, with our cawkin' seagulls an' chatterin' choughs. Come, tell us, how did all this beauty end?

JOSH: It has not ended, never ended, but you know the way of the world? The world is not these birds we speak of. Instead, it is a vulture and it circles and gnaws down on what it should love.

CHORUS: Too true, pard. But listen... How did you get your name? When the confusion of tongues occurred, how did your people name their world? We named our world with fish, tin and copper. Pesk, stean ha cober. What about you, boy Josh?

JOSH: For utter shame of me, I have near forgot. I only recall small phrases, odd words from my dear mother. Then, when they came for me, all of that ended. They gave me my first name: Joshua – from the Bible. The successor of Moses. He led the exodus from the River Jordan into Canaan. A traveller, just like me, so 'twas apt. I had no first or last name. I explained that I was just Emi-dee. A man wrote it down. That was when... That was when all altered... when he wrote it down. The stories stopped. The birds scattered. The forest was never the same. There were ghosts of families still walking our paths, but they had gone. [*Pause*] We sold ourselves. Do you know that, jowster women?

CHORUS: We know so little Emid-ee. Enlighten us…

JOSH: Dinaa dem. I will go soon. They will come for me.

CHORUS: Who comes, berimbau boy?

JOSH: Slavers. They look like you. They have your milky skin.

CHORUS: [*incredulous*] Like us?

JOSH: From lands north of here. Another ocean people. They have white sails tall as the jungle and sticks that roar blasting fire.

CHORUS: [*menacing*] Why do you run?

JOSH: I run to escape. Not to be taken. To stay free…

2. The Slavers

The CHORUS *transforms into the slavers. Berimbau music becomes louder and more frantic. A choreographed chase follows, which culminates in* JOSH *being pulled from side to side. The* CHORUS *holds him in a crucifix position, his arms outstretched.*

The CHORUS *slowly sniffs his body and touches him in a erotic way.* JOSH*'s arms are kept up and then bound to a tree branch. His feet are then chained.*

CHORUS: Traga o bastardo negro com voce. Vigie para que ele nao fuja. Cuidado com o ele diz. [*Pause*] Se você quer culpar alguém pelo seu destino, culpe seus próprios reis. Foram eles que te venderam por utensilios de cozinha, por animales domesticos, por sementes, graos e rum!

JOSH: Hear them, these Portuguese. Pity them. They know not what they do. They do what they think is their right, ever since one Antão Gonçalves first claimed us for bonded labour. Among my people his name rings like a demon. And now here come his progeny to the Gold coast. [*Pause*] Oh yes – unbelievers make fine slaves. It is the ruling principle of their people. But then, slavery is nothing new my friends. Yes – we slave ourselves to ourselves.

At the end of this speech, a member of the CHORUS *harshly punches* JOSH *in the stomach so that he doubles up in pain.*

CHORUS: Feche acima o ralé!

JOSH: They bundle us, make us walk in lines tied to poles, then push us into slave castles. These are no towers rising in the air, but instead stinking pits in the ground, filled with filth. There is no food. Many die of disease and malnutrition. [*Pause*] I stay there until it is time to be transported. How have our gods allowed this to happen to us? What wrong did we commit? [*Looks up*] From our hole, we see above muskets, cloth, gunpowder and metals – gifts for our leaders: men who should have protected us. See this double evil then. Slavers, and men who'd sell their own to slavers. Spend your money, my kings. Fire those weapons you won. Drink the alcohol you have earned. The music here is the moaning of men and women. The melody is fear and betrayal. My soul craves other sounds. And these Portuguese are supposed to be Christians. Before we leave, they baptise us. The English laugh at them. "Why bother?" they say. "You'd be better off baptising apes..." I am no ape. I am a man!

The CHORUS *takes a bowl of water and makes the sign of the cross upon* JOSH*'s head.*

CHORUS: Logo no princípio do mundo, o vosso Espírito pairava sobre as águas, para que já desde então concebessem o poder de santificar.

JOSH: There I was sleeping. I woke up from a dream, and suddenly I was a Christian. They named me Joshua.

Pause.

CHORUS: Você começou feriados em Brasil.

JOSH: So, I journey. I am the Odysseus of music. Manillas and cowrie shells are exchanged, and traders load us on board the first of many ships I would come to know. No river canoes these, but huge ocean-going cities of human cargo. I am fifteen years old; enough of a man to know inhumanity. Guinea bled. A third of us die. I don't know how I survived. I remember the smells: piss, shit, blood, sick, the stinking fish they fed us on. I hear women giving birth, children suckling their mother's milk, the elders coughing, the sounds of men going mad. [*Pause*] Through the slits in the timber, I spy five other ships – equally full of men and women. Have you tried dancing in chains? I try it when I hear the melodies above – coming from the captain's quarters. It leaves cuts on your ankles, scrapes the bone raw. In all this, the slavers' faces become skulls you wish to smash. I know how an animal must feel. Such caging, such submission, creates hatred in the heart. It sears into the soul.

CHORUS: Off Brazil was 'ee?

JOSH: The Americas, yes. Not the Hy Brasil of your fables either. Instead, the southern lands, where they say strange devils walk in the forests, and men hunt each others' heads. I am bound for labour in the sugar or tobacco plantations there. Tell me, jowster maids, just how many of my people were taken? Do you know? Do your history books tell you?

CHORUS: We have heard tell of two hundred and twenty thousand.

Pause.

JOSH: Truly, this is my land's devastation. Words, song, stories, music plucked up and tossed into the air... One day, I will write this. One day, I shall make music that tells it. One day, there will be a music that shall turn hearts.

CHORUS: We believe you Josh. But tell us about Brazil... Is there dancing there?

JOSH: [*enthusiastic*] Much dancing, fish-maids.

CHORUS: Show us then, so we may learn and embrace it. It is part of you and we wish to know all your drolls and tales.

JOSH: Crab-girls, I show you.

3. Minas Gerais, Brazil

Brazilian music. JOSH *shows the* CHORUS *a set of dance moves, which are then copied by the* CHORUS. *The moves are a fusion of Brazilian Rio de Janeiro carnival and typical Cornish processional. The fusion facilitates the incorporation of hip-hop moves and flips, as well as percussion, using the clogged feet of the* CHORUS. *The dance continues while* JOSH *is speaking.*

JOSH: Brazil is the new world. The old lines are less well-drawn, the etching less deep. When I landed, I was fearful at first. So many new people, such strange plants and animals, and me bonded in chains. Thank God, there are birds, plying their secret languages and melodious songs: leaf-tossers and puff-birds, pygmy-owls and quetzals, macaws and tanagers, parakeets and spoonbills. They fire my soul again, which for too long was in dark place. I make a new berimbau from the biriba wood. I find cabaça gourds and play music again. I take tunes I know from home. I fuse them with these new rhythms of the jungle, even with the sets the sailors play.

JOSH *plays the berimbau. The dancing stops and the* CHORUS *listens again.*

CHORUS: Are you still bound?

EDUARDO SOUTO DE MOURA *enters.*

JOSH: Always in chains, maidens. But I do not go to the plantations.

EDUARDO: What is that escravo?

JOSH: ...asks a man in Rio de Janeiro. "Josh Emidy," says my captor.

EDUARDO: He has a noble appearance... Though he is black, the brow is less pronounced, the jawbone smaller.

JOSH: Who is this man? A Bandeirante, an adventurer who has found gold and diamonds in the Minas Gerais. Oh yes, these are the mines which will pay off European debts – with the blood of slaves. I look at my hands, and think that these fingers which nimbly pluck berimbau string must now become shovels deep underground. Fear finds me again, and lands upon my shoulder. I am bid for, and sold to Eduardo Souto de Moura. We travel miles on a cart into the mountains, and there for the first time, I am given trousers...

JOSH *struggles to put on a pair of trousers.*

JOSH: I knew nothing of such garments.

EDUARDO: I will make you a gentleman...

JOSH: ...says this man to me. "Will I work the mine?" I want to ask. But he has grander plans for me. I am to be his man-servant – and second fiddle. First, he learns me Portuguese so I may complete his bidding.

JOSH *comically steps closer to* EDUARDO.

JOSH: I am to stand next to him, when he inspects the finds at his gold-fields. I carry his bags.

EDUARDO *throws his bags at* JOSH.

JOSH: I am, apparently, fashionable. All the best-dressed gentlemen of Brazil have a young Negro impling by their side. At least there is food.

EDUARDO: Go to Emideo... Fetch me more roasted galinha...

JOSH: ...says he. So I nod and bow, and do what I am told. That way, I get to eat his leavings. Guinea becomes further away. I have days when I forget the faces of my mother and father. I no longer recall how my brother speaks. The African is becoming the Portuguese. Do you know that feeling jowsters? Do you have that in your land? [*Pause*] Losing your identity is worse than losing a limb. It keeps me awake. It stops me eating. I am praying to this new God with my master. He has built a church in the mountains. The congregation sing songs I could never have imagined. I look down into the valley and understand the beauty and sadness of it all. Jowsters, are you there? Are you there still?

CHORUS: We'm here. We'm with you.

JOSH: Answer me this: why so much change?

Pause.

CHORUS: This is the world's way, Josh Emidy.

JOSH: Will it ever be better?

Pause.

CHORUS: We dun't knaw. We'm no oracle. Nawbody knaws. Come, Emidy boy, tell us your tale... You've some droll on 'ee...

JOSH: Women... I don't know what happens... It is all such a long time ago... No, I remember... My master speaks...

EDUARDO: That instrumento that I have heard you play...

JOSH: You mean berimbau?

EDUARDO: It is rudimentar... o instrumento idiota. I want something better for you. I cannot have you dressed as my servidor when you play upon a stick. It looks not nice.

JOSH: See, good jowsters, that is how things change.

CHORUS: What did 'a give 'ee?

CHORUS *gathers interested, around* EDUARDO *and* JOSH.

EDUARDO: I give you this violino. Now you can learn to play for me...

EDUARDO *ritually passes* JOSH *a violin, followed by the bow. The* CHORUS *makes appreciative noises.*

CHORUS: Oooo.... 'Ere... Look at tha' dunnee... What a beauty... Thaas' more like ut... We d'have they back the 'wink down Lamorna...

JOSH: How do I play it?

EDUARDO *shows him how to play by placing the violin next to* JOSH*'s chin and stepping around behind him.*

EDUARDO: You hold it to your queixo, your chin. Then you run the bow across the four strings like this... Hold the strings to alter the tone. I play like a strangled gatito, but you Emidy... you will master this música. I know it.

JOSH *begins to play. He plays just one string – a plaintive melancholic tone.*

EDUARDO: [*frustrated and anxious*] Not just uma, Emidy. You play all the cordas, the strings.

JOSH *plays again; this time using all four strings. The tune is more melodic.* THE CHORUS *is looking at him.*

EDUARDO: See...

JOSH: [*to audience*] This white man's instrument, it hurts my hands.

EDUARDO: You practica, yes? Then the ladies here, they will like the música in my house. I invite them to my chambers for the dancing and then a little more... Then maybe they like a little bit of me too, yes?

EDUARDO *winks at the audience. He moves to one of the female members of the audience, while* JOSH *is acquainting himself with the violin.*

EDUARDO: You like um pouco de mim, yes? I show you my huge gold nugget, yes?

While this is happening, in frustration, JOSH *has dropped the violin and returns to the berimbau. He starts playing it again. Back from the audience,* EDUARDO *faces him.*

EDUARDO: O que é que há? Why you leave the violino?

CHORUS: 'Ee dun't like ut. 'Ee d'like that bit ov stick an' gourd better...

EDUARDO: The stick and the gourd?

CHORUS: 'Es. That there bit ov' stick an' gourd.

JOSH *stops playing the berimbau.*

JOSH: I can't play it. You know – with my people – if something is not natural, we do not give it any value...

EDUARDO *becomes angry, and tries to control his frustration. He paces the stage.*

CHORUS: [*conspiratorially*] Here, Josh boy... You'd better do somethun'. Old chap there d'look fierce as a jungle buckrat and you'm too slaw to catch a cold dinner. Can 'ee not see this is your ticket out ov here?

EDUARDO: Not natural? Not natural? But all the finest senhores of Brazil have an escravo negro who can play violin. What am I to do? Maybe one of you lovely women might be interested in the situação...

CHORUS: Not we, fur heaven's sake sire. We dun't knaw our musical arse before our elbow fur certain. We'm only gossiping, gabbling old fish maids. We cudn' even be sirens over Zennor...

EDUARDO: I know... I know... He needs a teacher. I will find him one...

CHORUS: FIND ONE WHERE? Did 'ee knaw you'm nearnly fifteen thousand feet up in the Minas Gerais? You're supply station's twenty miles away. You'd be better off givin' a long-nosed tapir singing lessons master...

EDUARDO: [*to himself*] Yes – I will definitely find him a teacher...

CHORUS: He's as deaf as a haddock an' naw mistake.

JOSH: Sir, very well. If you can find me such a teacher here, then I will learn.

EDUARDO: Magnifico! Now will I have the lovely ladies come to tea... and play games in my chamber...

EDUARDO *exits.*

CHORUS: So, who did 'a get?

JOSH: A man in Rio.

CHORUS: Mmm... Fancy.

JOSH: Not really, jowsters.

CHORUS: What 'a do?

JOSH: Showed me how berimbau and violin are just the same...

CHORUS: Hands hurt did 'um?

JOSH: Every day.

CHORUS: What wuz the grub like?

JOSH: Good. Fresh plantains...

CHORUS: Give 'ee callouses did ut?

JOSH: On my fingers yes – and in my mind.

CHORUS: Why's that?

JOSH: He taught me music. Strange symbols on paper.

CHORUS: Notes an' clefs an' that?

JOSH: Yes – notes. Clefs. Quavers and semi-quavers.

CHORUS: Neck 'urt did ut?

JOSH: Yes – I couldn't sleep for it aching.

CHORUS: Practice much?

JOSH: Five hours a day. Sometimes more.

CHORUS: What sort of music?

JOSH: Strange sounds. White men's music.

CHORUS: Any good?

JOSH: Names and songs I'd never heard before.

CHORUS: But any good wuz ut?

JOSH: Let me play for you.

CHORUS: Proper. Come on maids. Let's we have a listen to what Josh've been taught...

JOSH *assumes a more trained position, and begins to play. Compared to his previous effort, the transition is incredible. The* CHORUS*'s faces however, become agonised, as if in pain. They cover their ears.* JOSH *stops.*

JOSH: What's wrong?

Pause.

CHORUS: Call that a tune do 'ee?

Pause.

JOSH: I do. It is what I have been taught. I find it very pleasing to the ear. So does my master. He says it appeals to his lady visitors…

CHORUS: My 'andsome – God's honest truth – it do sound like a cat blawin' off down on Newlyn Quay after a dish ov stinkun' pilchards.

JOSH: Really?

CHORUS: 'Es – really, my lover. I've heard the baissly parrots in the jungle here sound sweeter ov a mornin'.

JOSH: What should I do to please you?

CHORUS: If you'n read music… 'ave a gake at this 'un.

The CHORUS *member produces a sheet of music from behind her back.*

JOSH: What is it?

CHORUS: A tune. From back home. None of yer fancy rubbish. This is our music. Music for people, like you an' us Josh. Play it and we'll dance.

Tenuously, JOSH *accepts the sheet music, places it on a music stand and the* CHORUS *forms a circle around him. At first, he does not play confidently, but then becomes more assured. The music is the 'Newlyn Fisherman's Reel'. The* CHORUS *performs a fusionist adaptation of the traditional dance. Compared to the former piece, the music is frantic, earthy, loud and noisy with the* CHORUS *taking off their clogs and using them percussively.*

CHORUS: Caw d'hell maid. I'm proper knacked after thaa'…

CHORUS*: Me too. Let's go back home fur a drop taa and a piece ov hevva cake.

The CHORUS *exit.*

JOSH: In life, I have come to think that beauty does not end. It just changes. A few months ago, I was chained and bound in the stinking hold of a ship. These simple women show me there is more to life. You've heard of the tin violin – but that's a long way off, and I must change again. My master is a not an evil man – just an opportunist. I hear him now. He is entertaining a lady – but neither he nor she have many clothes upon their backs. They make the sounds of love and I have been dismissed from my duties, now that the music of seduction has worked. This instrument is part of me now. It has become – I think – natural.

4. The Art of Capoeira

EDUARDO *enters in a state of undress: trousers around his ankles, carrying a large and very dusty bottle of port.*

EDUARDO: You still here?

JOSH: Still here master…

EDUARDO: Go see your friends. Do some of your funny negro fighting in the forest. Come my violinista, you have the whole day off… How's that for an escravo? The lady inside… she like me [*winks*]…

JOSH: So I go… I meet with others who are not from my village or land… but they are from Africa, so we understand each other. We play our capoeira. No – I don't expect you know capoeira. Maybe a little, but not much. The authorities here, they don't like us playing it. We do it in secret – away from the plantations, away from the mines. It is the only way. They think it is a symbol of our criminality; that we plan our escape. You know, if we are caught, they cut the tendons on the back of our feet. We do not care. We still work our dance though. It is our resistance. You know what I am saying? How we pass on our old culture. Those stories of Songhai and Tondibi. How we lift our spirits. Look at these two…

Two capoeira dancers enter. They are members of the CHORUS, *who mark the circle and then bow respectfully before each other.*

JOSH: See how they make the roda – the circle, for the sparring and the singing… See how it begins… I sing a taunt. We sing it now in Portuguese:

Voce diz que sabe tudo. Larantina sabe mas.
Ela sobre na parede. Uma coisa que voce nao faz.

[You think that you know everything. The lizard, she knows more.
She can climb up a wall. Something that you can't do.]

JOSH: Now I leave the violin, and return to berimbau. Watch…

A capoeira dance now ensues. Musical accompaniment is performed by JOSH *on berimbau. The dance starts gently but moves to a crescendo of the martial art with fluid acrobatic play, subterfuge, sweeps, non-contact kicks and ballet-like movement.*

JOSH: So you see the beauty, the grace of it. How gentle my people are...

The delicate movement continues. JOSH *stops playing. He notes the violin, and moves across to it.*

JOSH *looks at the audience, then back to two* CHORUS *dancers.*

Eventually he picks up the violin, and in the style of berimbau, adds traditional accompaniment. The moment is beautiful and tranquil.

This moment is broken by the arrival of the authorities (played by other members of the CHORUS*), who arrive with truncheons, batons and knives.*

CHORUS: This gathering is illegal! Round them up! Negro-fighting is banned... Beat them.

Chaos ensues. JOSH *drops the violin and its bow. The authorities and the capoeira dancers move to a freeze in which the beatings are shown.*

CHORUS: Cut their legs. Make them bleed.

The authorities produce knives and mime the cutting of tendons on the backs of the dancers' feet. The dancers fall in agony to the floor. Music: discordant from a violin's strings.

Initially JOSH *runs away off-stage, but he returns to pick up the violin and its bow. Lights fade down.* DANCERS *rise to complete the transition.*

Lights fade up. EDUARDO *enters in a state of nakedness. He realises he is naked and covers himself. A transition:* CHORUS *back into role of the Jowster women.*

EDUARDO: Where has he gone, women? Tell me.

CHORUS: We d'think the bugger 'av run off...

EDUARDO: Fugido? Escaped?

CHORUS: 'Ee wuz out of here quicker than duckshit, Master Souto de Moura.

EDUARDO: Does he have my violino?

CHORUS: Aw 'es sire. That wuz the first thing 'ee 'eaved in 'is sack. 'Ee wudn' goin' t'forget tha' now was 'a?

EDUARDO: Fetch my men and cachorros, dogs... Search the mine... Track him through the jungle. Have men at the port! Get chains ready! That violin cost me a fortune... I want it back. The price of the lessons – it nearly broke me... but then, he did help me get the ladies, yes? I need more ladies. I have to get him back...

One of the members of the CHORUS *eyes up* EDUARDO*'s crotch with a telescope.*

CHORUS*: My gar! I ebm' seen one like that fur a long time... 'Tis like a dogfish in May an' naw mistake! I wun' mind a bit ov that fur dinner...

She chases EDUARDO *off stage. He is full of fear and looks back at the audience in sheer horror.*

JOSH: So that's how I left. He wanted more ladies, but I wanted my freedom. I say goodbye to Eduardo Souto de Moura. My story is still young. It is still a small shoot in the rain forest, but do you see how it is growing? Now I have left my berimbau behind, and all I have is this violin. So where do I go? I make my way down from the Minas Gerais, through the steaming jungle. I head for the coast. I am told that there I might see Africa and maybe all might be well again.

CHORUS: Are 'ee sure of that?

JOSH: I wish I knew...

CHORUS: Dun't 'ee go back Josh. Always go forward...

JOSH: But I am African... I have to go back... It is how my people think.

Pause.

CHORUS: African. European. English. Portuguese. Brazilian. Cornish. None of ut should matter Josh Emidy. We'm all just people with the same problems. Heat. Food. Water. Sex. Death. They'm the things that count; the only things that d'matter.

JOSH: Where should I go? I don't understand my story.

CHORUS: Go where the music takes 'ee. Thaas' what I d'say.

5. The Harbour at Rio de Janeiro

The sound of the ocean and seagulls.

JOSH: So many boats... Where can they all be going?

CHORUS: Not back to Guinea, thaas' fur sure.

JOSH: I go with this one, then...

CHORUS: Has that boat got music? You need music to calm the tempests, to sooth the waves.

JOSH: My playing will be my passage. I am Odysseus once more.

CHORUS: Quick then boy Emidy. Get yourself on board.

CHORUS*: Knaw where 'ee's goin'?

CHORUS: 'Ebm got a clue! The old world somewhere I 'spect.

CHORUS*: Least 'tis away from here. I d'hate they baissly parrots.

Pause. The CHORUS *begin to close up tighter and start to gossip.*

CHORUS: 'Ere – what happened to him then – that Souto de Moura, the stallion ov the Amazon?

CHORUS*: Aw 'ee. That Eduardo? Well, I had my way wicked way widn'. Who didn'! 'Ee went and made a fortune...

CHORUS: I heard 'ee died of the pox...

CHORUS*: Aw 'es. Pity. Nothun' stays the same maid. Nothun' stays the same...

As they move into the shadows, the CHORUS *closes the act with the same haunting chant of words (in the Cornish language).*

CHORUS: Crowder... crowder... crowder...
Dean due... Dean due... Dean due...
Groudel... groudel... groudel...
Gweadar... gweadar... gweadar...
Haze gwaze... Haze gwaze... Haze gwaze...

Act Two

1. The Teatro do Solitre, Lisbon

The chant of 'Haze gwaze...' fades. Lights up. Carrying a wooden violin and bow, JAMES SILK BUCKINGHAM *steps onto stage, sits and speaks.*

JAMES: [*excitedly*] This remarkable man was one of the most finished musicians I ever heard, and I have had the privilege of hearing most of the celebrated performers who have graced the London stage during the past fifty years. Not one of them in my estimation has equalled this unknown Negro. He was not only a wonderful manipulator of the violin, but could write fluently many clefs; his hands seemed especially adapted for the work, his extremely long, thin fingers were not much larger than a goose quill; where this great talent came from was always a mystery to me, and to all who came in contact with him.

JAMES *exits. Lights fade. Portuguese guitar music. Lights up on centre stage.*

Music ends. A trumpeted fanfare (slightly out of tune at the end) greets the arrival of MARIA I, QUEEN OF PORTUGAL, *who is getting ready to go to the Teatro do Solitre in Lisbon.* MARIA *is a fairly elderly queen, who is prinked up in over-the-top make-up, to try to make her look younger. She has the mazed look of a crazed old aunty about her. The* CHORUS *are still wearing their jowster clothes, but now play the role of her courtly assistants.*

MARIA: [*screaming madly*] Ai Jesus! Ai Jesus! Ai Jesus!

CHORUS*: [*calm*] What ever is wrong, your majesty?

MARIA: I shall never be ready. Never be ready. Tonight I should never have had that dinner of barley and oyster stew... It has given me the fiery indigestion from hell [*burps*].

The CHORUS *provide pink clothing, and jewellery, add blusher and tie up her hair. A crown is placed on top of her head. This movement is completed as a piece of dance, with repetitive moves and symbols – as a kind of galliard. The* CHORUS *uses ribbon to thread* MARIA*'s costume around her.*

CHORUS*: Queen Maria, your physicians say it is good for you.

MARIA: Physicians ha! What do they know?

CHORUS*: They care for your health, your majesty.

MARIA: Absolute hypocrites the lot of them. They're all mad – what with their potions and compresses...

CHORUS*: Your majesty, do you require your dwarves for this premiere?

MARIA: No. No dwarves. Not tonight. You know I only take the dwarves out in daytime to show them off to the sweaty masses. Give them the day off and the rest of the oyster stew... They should be happy with that. [*Pause*] What have we tonight anyway? Is it one of those ranting prose tragedies? You know how I despise them... [*excited*] Is it pastoral or farce? I like these very much indeed.

CHORUS*: It is an opera...

MARIA: Opera...? Which one?

CHORUS*: A new one your majesty, based on the virtuous life of Cleopatra.

MARIA: Pah! No doubt full of stupid castrati taking the female parts, staggering around in front of wooden pyramids. They should let women act. We must be the only country in the whole of Europe who still don't let women on the stage.

CHORUS*: I am told this production is very good, ma'am. It is the debut of the Opera House's new violinist. A man of some measure, I am told. He is from Africa.

MARIA: Africa? Who cares!? I don't. Not a jot. Not a fig. One violin player is much like the next: fools with jutting chins and calloused fingers and the opera will be stuffed with all kinds of hob-e-di-hoy, tottering pansies on high-heeled shoes, warbling airs in fluted falsettos... The last thing I saw was a stout shepherdess in virgin white – with a beard! She, or he, had a fist that could knock down Goliath... Sophistication is what we need here in Lisbon. It needs to be less French and more

Italian…

The CHORUS *continues to ready* MARIA *with the same ritualistic movement.*

The stage is transformed into the lobby of the Teatro do Solitre. With suitable flourish, the CHORUS *rolls out a pathetically small red carpet.* JOSH *enters nervously. He is adjusting his formal musician's clothing, and so looks slightly uncomfortable. We see a new level of sophistication to his character.*

JOSH: See me now. Who'd have believed it? Playing with the Lisbon Opera. I have fallen on my feet; Lisbon is on the fringe of Europe, but it is the gateway to the new world – and the tin violin. All the great and the good come here.

MARIA: [*aside to the Chorus*] Is it that the bunch of ne'er-do-wells I am meant to meet?

CHORUS*: It is your majesty.

MARIA: What a shower!

CHORUS*: These are the great performers and musicians of the Lisbon Opera. It is has a justified reputation your majesty.

MARIA: Yes – and I am the Queen of Sheba…

Some of the CHORUS *hurriedly join* JOSH *in the theatre lobby line-up being presented to* MARIA. *The* CHORUS *adjust their clothes to try to look respectable. The* CHORUS *stays with* MARIA I *as her advisor.*

JOSH: That's how I came to be presented to the Queen. When the ship from Brazil docked in the River Tagus, I knew no one. I needed money. I was hungry. The only thing I had was Eduardo's violin. So I stood at the dock and played. Yes – I busked for my living. [*Pause*] An impressario spots me. Says I am talented. Asks where I'd learn to play. In Brazil, says I. You, my boy, are destined for great things, says he. So he buys me a meal in Rossio Square's finest restaurant. [*Pause*] Next day, I'm up for an audition with the Opera… The lead violinist – a bad tempered fellow I am told – has left the day before in an argument over his playing. Play, says the conductor; so I play. I play for five minutes and then he points… That is your seat, says he. Welcome to the Lisbon Opera. Of course, I am the only negro there. I am a novelty you might say; a freak of nature…

CHORUS*: Presenting her wondrous, most beautiful and most excellent majesty, Maria I, Queen Regent of Portugal and all her colonies.

CHORUS *and* JOSH *clap.* MARIA I *proceeds along the line-up.* CHORUS *members bow.*

MARIA: And what is your name... African?

JOSH: Josh Emidy, your majesty.

MARIA: And what pray, do you do?

JOSH: I play the violin.

MARIA: [*snobbish*] Really? The violin?

CHORUS*: I am told he is a virtuoso, ma'am. Gifted they say. His technical accomplishments dazzle the public.

MARIA: [*aside*] African virtuoso indeed! Whatever next? Cannibals singing coloratura... Pah! Lead me to my box. Oh, and make sure you've got plenty of Turkish delight... Me and my sweet tooth...! Ai Jesus... It'll ever be so...

JOSH: This Queen, they say, is mad. The broadsheets talk over her religious mania and melancholia... They say she lives in a pink palace and eats only barley and oyster stew, and Turkish Delight, indulging in conversations of a rather unchaste nature. Last week, someone said they had heard her running down the corridors naked shouting, 'Ai Jesus! Ai Jesus!' in a state of delirium, followed by such agonising shrieks one could hardly conceive possible. She fears half her family who have sworn vengeance against her. They say she has nightmares of foul phantoms. The only pleasure she still has in life, is perhaps music and confectionary...

MARIA: What do you mean no Turkish delight! Get the dwarves to bring some over from the palace...

MARIA *sits on a chair stage left. Another chair is on stage right. Here, enters* COMMANDER EDWARD PELLEW, *who looks at the audience, bows graciously before the queen, then sits.* MARIA *giggles, flirts and waves to* EDWARD *throughout the following sequence.* EDWARD *is reluctantly forced to acknowledge her.*

JOSH: So now you see how I must dazzle. Suddenly Josh Emidy is someone. See how the people gather. How they take their seats. I marvel at their finery. Guinea seems a universe away from me. And even Brazil… Some days I wake and my time there seems like a dream. See how they are curious about me. I am alien – but they want to see me play. Maybe too, they want to see me go wrong… I will show them though. I am as good as any player in the courts of Europe.

CHORUS*: You show 'em, Josh boy. We've always known you had ut in 'ee… ebm' us girls? Go on, pull yer string. Waggle yer bow…

JOSH: How do you find me here?

CHORUS*: Aw – you knaw we Cornish. Look all over the world, and we'll be there. And this hovel ov a theatre'll do fur we fur now…

JOSH: Jowsters, I must go. The performance will start soon.

CHORUS*: [*excitedly*] We cen't wait! We got front row seats!

JOSH: Look out for me.

Josh exits.

CHORUS*: Come on, maids. Let's get we down the front.

The CHORUS *moves to the front of the stage, pushing past and knocking into* EDWARD.

CHORUS*: 'Xcuse me… Sorry… 'Xcuse me… Sorry me bum's s'big… 'Tis all tha' saffron cake I d'eat…

The CHORUS *sits down with their backs to the audience. After they settle, they strike up a whispered conversation.*

CHORUS*: Want a mint imperial, do 'ee?

CHORUS*: Mmmm, lovely… My mouth's been dry as bootjack all day.

There is the sound effect of an audience settling down and an orchestra tuning up and then the tap of the baton of a conductor, who brings the players and audience to silence. The creation of this silence is important. A spot-lit JOSH *enters and stands before them. He begins to play. Here, a sound effect of an orchestra playing the overture, which highlights* JOSH*'s playing. Music fades to an operatic voice, over which* JOSH *speaks.*

JOSH: People, can you believe this? I can't. These singers convey such drama. Sometimes when I am playing, I think, if only they knew my story. That would make some opera. I love watching the performance from the orchestra pit. Ha – a bit different than those pits my people were thrown into as slaves. Much has changed. The libretto, the acting, the scenery, the costumes, the dancing... It all thrills me. Here, in Lisbon the audiences want Mozart, Mozart, Mozart. But one day, I would like to write an opera. That is my dream... How far can this slave rise? Can I fuse all that I have learnt into art? You know, perhaps I can.

JOSH *puts his violin to his chin and plays again. It is a beautiful virtuoso violin solo, underpinned by glorious operatic singing. The rest of the* CHORUS *completes a comic mime of an interpretation of the opera. A* CHORUS *pair speaks over this.*

CHORUS*: I tell 'ee dear. This d'properly float my boat... You dun't get this back Redruth Institute...

CHORUS*: You'm right there, maid. Nor over Trura neither. That Emidy – 'ee idn' no ordinary fool...

EDWARD *tries to stop them from talking.*

EDWARD: Shhhhh!

CHORUS*: Shhhhh... yourself y'fitcher! Want another mint imperial, do 'ee?

CHORUS*: Hey – who's the boy over there dressed up like a 'oss marine with a g'eat gannet of a hairdo?

CHORUS*: Aw – 'ee. They d'say thaas' Commander Edward Pellew.

CHORUS*: Who's 'ee?

CHORUS*: Aw – some British naval officer... On the pull probably. Like they all are out 'ere.

CHORUS*: [*giggling*] Dishy idn' 'a? I tell 'ee what. I wudn' mind a length ov 'is yard-arm any day ov the week!

CHORUS*: Looks like that mad Maria d'like 'un too... She'm passun' 'un over pieces ov Turkish Delight, look...

JOSH *finishes playing and bows. Here, the sound effect of a large audience clapping.* JOSH *bows again, waves and exits.*

CHORUS*: Look at Josh getting the applause. He's tickled up ass now. He's set fur life and naw mistake.

EDWARD: Bravo! Bravo! Bravo... I say – that negro can't half play.

The CHORUS *throws bouquets of flowers and rose petals at* JOSH*'s feet.*

EDWARD: See those women...[*points to Chorus*] These foreign types seem to go for a man in uniform. It sets their blood racing, you see. That, and the dashed prickly heat. They like a bit of stiff upper lip... I never rise to it of course. Always keep myself in check. Her majesty has been passing me sweets. [*Pause*] As if she thinks a splendid chap like myself would even contemplate a night of Turkish delight with her...I've heard all about her pink palace. No. I've got more important things on my mind: strategies against the French. Those conniving garlic-eating Gallic clowns who want to rule the seven seas...

CHORUS*: [*flirting*] A'right Commander Pellew... Now, woz a strapping man like you doin' at some pansy opera like this?

CHORUS: Stop 'ut y' boiled mackerel head... Commander Pellew don't care fur no lovin' from you – do 'ee now? I'm much more t'yur likin, bain't I Cap'n? I'll be the clotted cream on your jam split if y'like...

EDWARD *responds, but then ignores her and backs away scared.*

EDWARD: My frigate 'The Indefatigable' had to dock in the Tagus for repairs. So I thought I'd seek out some culture in the city, and found myself at the opera house. I don't give a jot for opera really. A lot of damned fools wandering around in tights is all I can see, with squeaky voices that grate harshly on the ears. [*Pause*] But the opera is where a man of my stature should be seen. As a representative of the King's Navy, one has to suffer for one's country. Give me a good rum and a jig on the foredeck any day. In fact, the men have been moaning that they've had no music for months. I need to sort that out or I'll have a mutiny on my hands... [*pause*] It seems that Queen Maria has taken a bit of liking to one's... er... shiny buttons and er... general nautical demeanour... Something we British officers have to deal with on a regular basis.

CHORUS *leaves, realising they haven't a chance. Seeing this failure,* MARIA *comes over. She hasn't a chance either, but this does not stop her trying.*

MARIA: [*sensual and husky*] Ai Jesus! Ai Jesus! Ai Jesus! Good Commander... You look very, very edible, yes... in your glistening uniform...

EDWARD: Delighted to meet you, your majesty.

MARIA: Would you like a little more tasty Turkish Delight, my little English sailor boy?

EDWARD: No. Not for me. Thank you. Have to keep trim. Life on the ocean wave and all that, what?

MARIA: [*flirting*] A fine performance tonight, wasn't it, Commander?

EDWARD: [*nervous now*] Yes. That violinist. Astonishing. Your – ah – husband, the King. Is he here tonight?

MARIA: That tolo! No, he will be at home asleep after making his love to his bottles of port... and then falling down the stairs the wrong way...

EDWARD: I see. Well, give him my felicitations won't you? And on behalf of the British Navy, thank him for Portugal's hospitality, and so on and so forth.

MARIA: [*moving closer, in for the kill*] I want your body Commander Pellew! You British excite me... You can put into my port any day. And the opera we have seen, this Antonio and Cleopatra... Ai! Be my Antonio... Grrrrr...

EDWARD: Yes. Dashed shame it all ended in tragedy. Well, better be shoving off...

MARIA: So soon Captain?

EDWARD: Sorry... Repairs done, I think. We sail at dawn.

MARIA: I like your priapic posturing, Commander Pellew. Can I not tempt you with the charms of the night?

EDWARD: No. [*Pause*] No charms, thank you very much.

MARIA: What if I am a little bit more persuasive? After all, this is my city and my country. It is – how you say in Britain, a custom. Ai Jesus, we would consider it rude! Now, men, draw your swords...

The CHORUS *transform into* MARIA*'s guards and all surround* EDWARD, *putting their hands around his neck.* EDWARD *is shocked and meekly complies.*

EDWARD: Well, your majesty, as you put it like that, perhaps we should share the pleasures of the boudoir together? I could show you my heroism under fire...

MARIA: Ai Jesus! Now he will see my pink palace...

The CHORUS, MARIA *and* EDWARD *exit.* MARIA *pinches* EDWARD*'s rear and turns to wink at the audience. We hear their voices off stage.*

EDWARD: Now, what did you say the name of that violinist was? Rather good wasn't he?

MARIA: He is named Emidy. Josh Emidy.

[*Maria offers Edward more Turkish Delight*]

EDWARD: Oh yes... some more Turkish Delight would be perfectly splendid...

MARIA: Yes, a little delight for both of us I think [*giggles childishly*].

2. The backstreets of the city

Enter JOSH, *back in his regular clothing, carrying his bag, bow and violin.*

JOSH: Ah – the best feeling in the world... into the air of the night. Did you see the bouquets and flowers? Everywhere in Lisbon is the tinkling of night-time guitars. It is when the people awaken. And now I feel awakened. I have found myself. And do you know? Tonight I am offered another position – at the Carlos theatre. A new opera by Cimarosa. Outside in the early hours, I like to watch the stars above and wander though the white marble city. The youth of the town light fireworks and I feel alive again. Lisbon is a place I think I could live in for the rest of my life. Maybe one day I will earn enough to return to Guinea and see what remains of my people there. The money I earn here can help us – make our lives better...

As JOSH *speaks members of the* CHORUS, *now hooded, and playing a Naval Press Gang sneak up upon him from behind. They are armed with truncheons and rope.* JOSH *notices their movement and backs away.*

JOSH: Who are you?

CHORUS: [*sinister*] Y'dun't need t'knaw Emidy...

JOSH: Get away from me, you rake-hells...

CHORUS: We'm no rake-hells boy. We'm the British Navy...

JOSH: What do you want?

CHORUS: [*menacing*] Well, a tune on that fine fiddle of yours would go down well... very well indeed. A bit of pressing is what we'm seekin', boy...

JOSH: Go back into the shadows you have come from, you devils.

JOSH *tries to run, but at each turn he is blocked by a member of the* CHORUS.

CHORUS: Tidn' no good y'dean due! You'm ours. We got our orders. Pellew gived us a list when 'ee got back. Slammed his door on his antics with that there Queen Maria... and told us where you might be...

JOSH: Pellew?

CHORUS: Aye. Commander Pellew. Saw you at the operatics tonight. Said you might fit the bill. Stupid enough. Daft enough t'be wanderin' these here dangerous streets at night. Rope him boys... Stuff him full of rum... 'Ee won't remember a thing...

In a ritualistic way, the CHORUS *members wrap rope around* JOSH *and harshly tie his hands. They force rum down him. This movement is completed as a dance. He is pushed to the ground, beaten with the truncheons and then lifted and carried out by the* CHORUS. *The music here is a repeat of the African motif found at the start of the play. It is combined with the violent beating of the* CHORUS*'s clogs on the floor. Lighting changes to red.*

CHORUS: [*snarling*] What you all gakin' at? This is enlightened Naval recruitment. Got a problem with that 'ave 'ee? [*picking on a male individual in the audience*] We've plenty of room fur more. You'n come too if you like, boy? Got a beauty job fur 'ee scrubbin' the heads...

This CHORUS *member kneels down, to pick up* JOSH*'s violin.*

CHORUS: [*with evil*] Ha! Ha! Ha! The boy'll be needin' tha'...

CHORUS *re-enter with* JOSH *born aloft (as if being taken toward a cannibal's cooking pot) and ironically singing the traditional Cornish song 'The Press Gang'. The* CHORUS *carry* JOSH *around the stage, and if possible in and out of the audience and around the performance space.*

CHORUS: [*singing*] Hi! Ha. Too-ra, loo-ra, loo-ra loo!
Hi! Ha. Too-ra, loo-ra, loo-ra loo!
Then amang um oll they took me up,
An lugg'd me down to a boat,
When ses the measter to the men,

"Let's see the rascal afloat!"
But then I begg'd un in good steed,
An I look'd like anything
That they shudd'n tip me in the sea,
But send me to sarve the King.
Hi! Ha. Too-ra, loo-ra, loo-ra loo!
Hi! Ha. Too-ra, loo-ra, loo-ra loo!
Now as we on the ocean sail'd,
We see'd a French ship comin';
Our Cap'n Pellew called oall ands to quarter,
And a feller went 'round drummin'
I beginn'd to coall ovver my past life,
My sinful actions oall
"Aw dear!" says I, "ef I shud die,
What wud become o' my soul?"

The CHORUS *carries* JOSH *off stage. Their song fades.*

Hi! Ha. Too-ra, loo-ra, loo-ra loo!
Hi! Ha. Too-ra, loo-ra, loo-ra loo!

3. The Indefatigable

Bright blue light. The sound of the sea: waves, seagulls and someone being piped aboard. EDWARD *is in his officer's quarters on board 'The Indefatigible'.* EDWARD *finds a Turkish Delight box and hides it, shaking his head and checking himself. Mumbles to himself: 'Lucky escape that one!' Once disposed of, he uses a chart and compass, with sextant. There is a knock at the door.*

EDWARD: Come…

CHORUS: 'Ere he be sir.

EDWARD: 'Ere he be sir? What kind of speak is that, sailor? 'Here he is', sailor. 'Here he is'. I insist upon the right pronunciation. Shake off the shackles of your pathetic Penryn upbringing, boy.

CHORUS: [*nervous*] Yes sir. I will try to do my b…b…b…b… best.

EDWARD: Who do you have for me?

CHORUS: We found 'un, zir.

EDWARD: Found 'un sir! Confound you man. 'We found him sir'.

CHORUS: Sorry zir.

EDWARD: Who?

CHORUS: That there negro fiddler, zir.

EDWARD: Emidy?

CHORUS: 'Es. That's 'is name.

EDWARD: Fetch him in.

CHORUS: Aye, aye, zir.

The CHORUS *exits to fetch* JOSH.

EDWARD: Yes, I'm a Cornishman, but I don't like to think about it too much. It gives me palpitations, you know... I've left all that behind me. Well, one has to speak properly. One has to, to get on. [*Pause*] Why speak with the ugly dialectical intonations of some dung-encrusted farmer from Penwith when one can use the King's English. I make a point of it, running 'The Indefatigable'. I'll have no swearing and no proper-job cakey-head, dabbered-up, emmety, figgy-hobbin, tiddy-hoggan, alright-my-handsome-beauty-wozon-my-lover-type shenanigans on my watch. Let's have the prepositions and the past participles in all the right places. I am a veritable precision for it. And any member of the crew who even tries speaking Cornish, I'll have them clapped in irons and flogged round the fleet, and fed on mouldy bread and dripping for a week. We've no place for that stupid tongue in the modern era. English helps, especially with these foreign types. When we splendid British speak our splendid English tongue, everyone jumps to attention. That is why our navy is second to none and why my command is rated among the best in the British Navy. [*Pause*] Now, let's see what this swish-swasher Emidy has to say for himself...

The CHORUS *enters with* JOSH, *who is roped up.*

JOSH: [*angry, exasperated and struggling against his captor and the ropes*] Why did you take me?! Have I not already been taken from my true home?! And when I find one I like, I am hounded again...

EDWARD: Look, it's nothing personal old chap. I saw you playing last night. You're quite a talent. I need a musician on board. You fitted. We're a bit short-staffed at the moment what with French cannon-balls and the occasional overboard leap, scurvy, or a drop of yellow fever. Some get pushed. And usually a few tend to get left behind wherever we put in. High turnover, I suppose you'd call it. That's the modern world for you. Nobody's ever happy. You'd think them being forced to join the British Navy would be the blessed highlight of their mediocre lives.

JOSH: So, Captain, I am to be torn from an orchestra to be your foredeck fiddle player?

EDWARD: I suppose that's one way of looking at it. Pressing people is the only way you see. Standard practice, that's all. Any port in a storm...

JOSH: I had...

EDWARD: Yes? Had what exactly?

JOSH: ... a life there.

EDWARD: Yes. But you were still bonded man weren't you? I mean, did the orchestra pay you the going rate?

JOSH: I was paid well.

EDWARD: Mmmm. You weren't on a white wage. I know that for a fact.

JOSH: I had enough. That was all I needed.

EDWARD: Well, you'll be kept well here on board. The King's Navy value musicians, you know. Keeps the crew's morale up – that sort of thing. Like the sea-hags; the women below: when the men need a bit of slappy-tickly 'female' comfort. Know any good jigs do you?

JOSH: What are these... jigs?

EDWARD: Jigs? You know yo-ho-ho and a bottle of rum type shenanigans. Lots of uppy-downy stippy-stappy fiddle-playing so the chaps on board can dance. This sort of thing...

EDWARD *dances, showing the least graceful version of a jig ever performed.*

JOSH: You mean like my people's capoeira?

EDWARD: No, no. Not your weird little negro games. Look, I know you can read music. Try this book... Talk to the men on the decks below...

EDWARD *hands* JOSH *a book.*

JOSH: [*reading with some degree of difficulty*] 'Their Lordships of the

Admirality Complete Compendium of Official Jigs, Hornpipes and Skylarkings of His Majesty's Navy: Volume 1 – Acheans, Awake! to Dorothy Beach-head's Delight...'

CHORUS: You'll need this... Hands to dance and skylarks an' tha'...

The CHORUS *hands* JOSH *his violin and bow.*

EDWARD: Now run along. Don't fiddle while Rome burns – or rather do fiddle when we weigh anchor...

JOSH: Where are we going? Where will we end up?

EDWARD: Oh – Galicia maybe. Put into Corunna, then up the Bay of Biscay to the Channel, now the breach in our hull's repaired. We've the class you see Emidy. 26 long 24-pounders on the main deck. Two long 12-pounders and 18 42-pound cannonades on the quarter deck and fo'c'stle. That's 46 guns. 330 men and boys. I think it's time for a bit of Frenchy action... Masters, unfurl the sails. Let's put to sea... Fire the gun. Loose the foretopsail and then make signal for a convoy.

4. The Battle

JOSH *sits to study the Compendium, ploughing through the volume. After looking at a page, he puts bow to the violin, and on stage, the* CHORUS *swings into action, miming various activities and tasks on board the frigate. If possible, have a small beam which is swung across the stage area, to which is attached a sail. The* CHORUS *repeats the Cornish-language chant again.*

CHORUS: Crowder... crowder... crowder...
Dean due... Dean due... Dean due...
Groudel... groudel... groudel...
Gweadar... gweadar... gweadar...
Haze gwaze... Haze gwaze... Haze gwaze...

This chant builds into a work-song, which ends when EDWARD *comes on to inspect the deck of the ship.*

EDWARD: I hope I wasn't hearing any corrupting cuttle-fishing Cornish then, was I?

CHORUS: Crowder... crowder... crowder... [*suddenly stops*] No sir... That was some words Emidy taught us. From Africa. Wasn't it Josh?

JOSH: Er... what?

CHORUS: They there words… From Africa, weren't they?

JOSH: [*realising the* CHORUS *are in trouble*] Yes… um… from my homeland: Guinea.

EDWARD: Good. Good. We'll have none of that calamitous Corny clap-trap on my vessel…

EDWARD *inspects the* CHORUS*'s work.* JOSH *is reflective.* EDWARD *returns to his quarters, and we see him eating luxurious food.*

JOSH: So now I am part of this ship's complement. Reduced to a number: 316. I am a Landsman – the lowest rating. A mere 16 shillings a month. [*Pause*] So, yes, I must learn the jigs but still man the guns as a blue powder monkey, work the rigging, haul the anchors. I am, in British Navy parlance, 'a volunteer'. My food is rationed: the Victualling Board's recommendations: a daily pound of bread and a gallon of beer. Weekly four pounds of salt beef and two pounds of pork, together with pease, oatmeal, butter and cheese! I ate so well in Portugal. Better still in Brazil where there was fruit. Here, there are just weevils and rats who eat better than we do… I grow thin again, while Pellew seems to eat more than the Queen of Portugal….

CHORUS: Where 'ee goin' then Josh?

JOSH: We've been patrolling the French coast from Normandy to Brittany… We captured the 'Virginie' without any loss of life or injury to our crew. Pellew has a fine a reputation now and earns splendid rewards from those vessels he's captured.

EDWARD: Emidy was doing well. He'd played me a few jigs: the last one was 'Raptures for a Jolly Tar'… What a fine tune! Oh, but never mind the music. I have to get on with the ship's log. [*Takes a quill to his log-book*] 14 January 1797. Fresh, breeze and hazy? Past noon saw a large sail made. [*Speeds up*] All sail in chase. 10 past 4 the chase carried away the main and fore top mast. [*More frantic*] 5pm hoisted our colours and fast moved to engage…

The CHORUS *makes the ka-boom noise of the attack, with cannon balls slamming into the sides of both vessels, and some falling into the sea. The* CHORUS *also makes the sounds of loading the balls, prompting the charge and the fuses hissing. We see* JOSH *drop his fiddle, to move to the cannons and work with the rest of the* CHORUS.

JOSH: ...with the pride of the French fleet, the 'Droit de l'Homme'. 74 guns on her, and she laid into us hard and fast... I was on the cannonades. No time for music; only the deafening recoil of the quarterdeck.

The CHORUS *continues with the noise and chaos of the broadsides.*

EDWARD: So we set everything we had into her. The engagement went on until twenty past four in the morning until 'The Amazon' came and supported and we were able to secure our masts and rigging [*The Chorus pulls the mast around*]. As we pulled round, we learnt that 'The Amazon' saw breakers on the Droit de l'Homme's bow, and that she was without mast. The day was finally ours. When dawn broke, she was sinking.

A mime, in which the CHORUS *and* JOSH *pretend to be bailing out. The mime should show that the bailing out is useless.*

JOSH: It was Pellew's day alright, but there was chaos below. We were up to our bellies in sea-water, and some of the guns had broken their breeches, tearing their ring-bolts from the sides. There was almost four feet of water in the hold.

CHORUS: Boy Pellew didn' give a monkeys about we in the wet. 'Ee was too busy prancin' around on the top deck and getting word to the Admirality that 'ee'd saved the day again. 'Twas running weth wet, you. Worse than the levels back Ding Dong Mine...

JOSH: Leastways we never foundered nor wrecked. Nor did any of the powder kegs go off when the enemy attacked.

CHORUS: Now, say what you like about Pellew...

CHORUS*: How about... 'He's a right knobber'.

The CHORUS *looks disapprovingly at the other* CHORUS *member.*

CHORUS: ... but the boy d'knaw how t'celebrate. He doubled the rum ration, and when we'd got things dry again, he ordered...

EDWARD: ... a celebration!

JOSH *drops his bucket and picks up his violin. The* CHORUS *begin clapping and stamping and* JOSH *plays a classic* CORNISH *jig. The playing and dancing are fusionist and frenetic. The* CHORUS *leads the festivities, while* EDWARD *gaily claps only.*

CHORUS: Come on Cap'n Pellew. I'll make a man ov ee yet...

EDWARD: A man of me you mean, surely?

CHORUS: Stop talkin' like you'm the First Sea Lord and get on an' party…

CHORUS plants a big kiss on EDWARD, who dances the jig in the most priggish way possible. JOSH moves around the stage and into the audience. The CHORUS dances wildly and shout and scream. Eventually, the CHORUS surrounds JOSH and EDWARD and then pushes them forwards, towards the audience.

5. The Sighting of Kernow

The jig stops. The CHORUS, JOSH and EDWARD look out towards the audience.

CHORUS: Is tha' what I think 'tis?

CHORUS*: 'Es. The promised land.

CHORUS: What, Kernow?

CHORUS*: 'Es. The land ov the West Britons… Cakey old place, that is.

The CHORUS screams with delight.

CHORUS: Proper job… We'm back home me 'andsomes… Les' go over Arwennack Street fur a bit of shoppin'. I got vouchers t'spend… an' money off coupons…

JOSH and EDWARD are left alone on stage.

JOSH: Where is this place?

EDWARD: Falmouth.

JOSH: Foul mouth…?

EDWARD: No. Falmouth. It's a harbour. The best in Britain. Deep water. Nothing foul about it at all.

JOSH: What must I do there?

EDWARD: Do what you like lad. Find your liberty. You're no longer part of the ship's company. Parliament's decided. The law's altered. Some emancipation for you. I've no choice but to set you free. Go on… It's a friendly enough sort of place…

JOSH: And you?

EDWARD *stands in Admiral mode.*

EDWARD: Promotion. Portsmouth. Up before the Commission. Should be an Admiral by the end of the month after that little spot of fisticuffs we had. I'm to be in charge of a line of battle...

JOSH: [*deadpan*] Congratulations.

EDWARD: Thank you. Oh – one word of advice. Watch out for the Cornish. A fine people last time I looked – but somewhat devious at times. Don't trust them as far as you can throw them. And make sure you get them to speak English... otherwise they'll go off in the most orotund circumlocutions...

JOSH: I'll be careful.

EDWARD: Off you pop then... The gangplank's just there...

JOSH *moves towards the gangplank to leave 'The Indefatigable'. He has forgotten his violin.*

JOSH: I'll be seeing you...

EDWARD *is vainly sizing up himself, strutting around and mouthing 'Welcome Admiral Pellew! My, you look absolutely splendid'. There is a brief moment where* EDWARD *thinks. He turns back to* JOSH.

EDWARD: I'm sorry.

JOSH: [*puzzled*] Sorry?

EDWARD: Sorry for what we did to you... how we took you...

EDWARD'*s words are unexpected.* JOSH *is frozen.*

EDWARD: All that roping, and rum and... er... Hi! Ha. Too-ra, loo-ra, loo-ra loo-ish sort of thing...

JOSH: I've had worse.

EDWARD: Yes. I suppose you have. Rum state of affairs really...

Pause.

EDWARD: . Find yourself here, boy. You are an original you know Emidy. I knew that from the first time I saw you in Portugal. History'll say it, and so do I...

JOSH *only nods and walks off stage. The* CHORUS *enters.*

CHORUS: Crowder… crowder… crowder…
Dean due… Dean due… Dean due…
Groudel… groudel… groudel…
Gweadar… gweadar… gweadar…
Haze gwaze… Haze gwaze… Haze gwaze…

EDWARD *notices he has left his violin behind.*

EDWARD: Damn fool. He's forgotten his…

EDWARD *runs after him shouting.*

EDWARD: Emidy! Emidy! Your violin… Dammit. He's gone.

EDWARD *exits.*

Act Three

1. Falmouth Harbour

The CHORUS *is busy moving chattels to and fro. The background music is now 'Celtic' and atmospheric. Over this, the* CHORUS *are chanting still. Into this, briskly enters* JAMES SILK BUCKINGHAM.

JAMES: Emidy began by going out to parties to play the violin, which he did to a degree of perfection never heard before in Cornwall; yet always with a most curious instrument: a violin made of tin. He swore it gave the most melodious tone. This led to his being engaged as a teacher, and then as leader of concerts; so that by degrees he made rapid progress in reputation and means. Soon with, great éclat, he became the leader of the Harmonic Society of Falmouth, held each month in the Town Hall.

JAMES *exits. In between the movements of the* CHORUS, *walks* JABEZ PENDER. JABEZ *is blind and taps the ground with a white stick held in his right hand. He is hooded, but under the hood wears the felt hat and candle of a tin miner. In his left hand, he carries a sack which obviously contains something of value. He keeps this close to his body.* JABEZ *mumbles a combination of tramp-like talking-to-yourself / fight-yourself Cornu-English and Cornish in which only a few words are intelligible, and shuffles around the stage.*

JABEZ: Yeah, yeah. Crowder stean. Stupid buggers. Gerrock. Clizzard. Fickia! Liggan. Poetherick. Beauty. Starry-gazzy. Spoom. Fickia! [*laughs*] Tol-a-mean. Sebbard. You party. Curwillet. Barvas. Fickia! Booger. Caggle. Away t'go. Gudgin. Maglen. Fickia. Scath. Morgul. Udjackapiffy. Hewer. Fickia! Cowl rooz. Guzalezza [*laughs*]. Yeah, yeah. Es. Annet. Bulgroneck. Fickia! Timmynoggy. Wherrick. That idn' right t'all. Bremming. [*Dirty laugh*] Fickia! Blowster. Emmet. Gerbeak. Cokyn-baba. [*Even dirtier laugh*] Fickia! Leverack. Pinnick.

Giss on!

JOSH *enters this moment, eyes skywards, observing this new country.*

JABEZ: Crowder stean. Stupid buggers. Gerrock. Clizzard. Fickia! Liggan. Poetherick. Beauty. Starry-gazzy. Spoom.. Fickia! Tol-a-mean. Sebbard. You party. Curwillet. Barvas…

JOSH *accidentally bumps into* JABEZ.

JABEZ: Fickia!

JOSH: Sorry… I wasn't looking where I was going.

JABEZ: Yeah, yeah. What 'ee say, sebbard?

JOSH: Sorry… It was my fault I bumped into you.

JABEZ: Where you from, soas? You sound like you'm from Devon… Or Ireland? From there, are 'ee? You sound like you'm from there, yes…

JOSH: No. I'm from... [*thinks*] Well… I'm from all over the place.

JABEZ: English, are 'ee? Silly buggers they are… They'm usually all over the place. Dun't knaw their ass from their elbow, they dun't. Yeah, yeah.

JOSH: No. From Africa [*pause*] first of all.

JABEZ: Africa? Af… rica? That south of the Lizard idn' ut? One ov they g'eat rocks that d'wreck ships…

JOSH: No… Yes... A long way from here, anyway.

JABEZ: Let me touch you… Explosives took out me eyes, you. In the mines see, back Creegbrawse… A goodly mine that… Plenty of fine tin there… Yeah, yeah.

JABEZ *touches* JOSH*'s face tenderly, feeling his brow and chin.*

JABEZ: [*slow*] I tell'ee sumthing fur nothun': [*quick*] You b'aint Cornish. You'm too bleddy andsome t'be one ov we… Fickia! Clizzard… what brings you here then?

JOSH: I was dumped here, off 'The Indefatigable'.

JABEZ: 'The Indefatigable'…? Udjackapiffy… That be Commander Pellew's vessel bain't ut? Knaw 'un did 'ee? Fulla' piss an' vinegar 'ee is.

JOSH: He was the man who captured me… then freed me…

Pause.

JABEZ: What, slave was 'ee? Where to?

JOSH *does not answer.*

JABEZ: Fickia. Yeah. yeah. You dun't have t'say… I'm Jabez. Jabez Pender. From the Penders of Porthinnis … And you?

JOSH: Emidy. Josh Emidy. Good to meet you Jabez. What brings you here then – to the docks I mean? Do you seek passage to the Americas?

JABEZ: [*amused*] Me! By gar… I dun't intend on goin' anywhere. I'm just lookin' thaas' all…

JOSH: Looking? What do you seek?

JABEZ: [*serious*] For the right one.

JOSH: I don't understand.

JABEZ: Prophecy, see. I'm the custodian: [*mumbles*] 'Seek 'ee down the sea the due dean, and give t'ee the crowder stean'.

JOSH: Look I must go… I must find lodging for the night…

JABEZ *shakes his head and laughs.*

JABEZ: Boy… you've no need to worry…Yeah, yeah. This here sack's what brought you here, across the miles. It've had your name written on it, oh, since before my grandfather was a boy…

JOSH: You speak in riddles.

JABEZ: No riddle. See, I've been the guardian for these long years now. But I'm no musician…

JABEZ *violently grabs* JOSH*'s hands and feels his fingers.*

JABEZ: …but these are the right hands. Player's hands bain't 'um?

JOSH: Yes.

JABEZ: I knawed ut. I knawed ut. Then this… is fur you.

JABEZ *hands over the sack.* JOSH *takes it.*

JOSH: What is it?

JABEZ: No folk-tale. No fairy tale. No droll. This is truth. You've the skill, but this... well, this'll help turn your skill to genius. [*Pulls Josh close*] There's magic in it.

JOSH: [*dismissive*] Magic?

JABEZ: 'Es. Good magic. The true magic of the Cassiterides. Now, mark my words. 'Twas right you left your fiddle on the frigate.

JOSH: What? How do you know?

JABEZ: I've been watchin'...

JOSH: But you're blind!

JABEZ: I can see in ways other men can't see... 'Twas meant to be. In this bag's your future. Play it. Compose upon it, and all'll turn to gold. Keep it with you 'til the end of your days.

JOSH: What is it?

JABEZ: You'll see.

Stage lights darken. Slowly, JOSH *pulls the object out of the sack. It is a tin violin and a bow. His complete focus is on these two objects. There is a spotlight on the tin violin so that its surface glimmers. The* CHORUS *stop their movements and as they chant,* JABEZ *nods knowingly, covers up his face and then slips away.*

CHORUS*: [*imitating Jabez*] Tol-a-mean. Sebbard. You party. Curwillet. Barvas. Fickia! Booger. Caggle. Away t'go...

JOSH: Where did you get it from?

CHORUS*: He be gone Josh. Went back Creegbrawse, fast as a long dog.

JOSH: Why's it made of metal?

CHORUS*: No trees in Cornwall boy. Their trunks be all underground, proppin' up the shafts and levels.

CHORUS*: [*in awe and pointing*] That there be the tin violin.

JOSH: [*incredulous*] A fiddle made of tin?

CHORUS*: 'Es. You got 'un...

JOSH: Do you think it really has magic in it?

CHORUS*: Only way to knaw is t'try it out.

JOSH: You're right.

JOSH *starts to play, but this time, no sound emerges from the violin. The playing is completed in slow-motion, and the* CHORUS *responds positively to the music. An expression of amazement crosses the face of* JOSH *and the faces of the* CHORUS.

CHORUS*: [*to audience*] That was beautiful... I'm ebm' heard anything like ut fur years.

CHORUS*: You wait 'til you hear ov ut. You'll be in cherks like a pig pissin'.

2. The Assembly Rooms, Truro

A transition: Lights bright to show change of location. The CHORUS *tidies up* JOSH *and makes him presentable. They comb his hair and put a tie on him.*

JOSH: I never saw Jabez Pender again, nor heard the droll of the violin's origin. I somehow found that its magical qualities made me play even better. I quickly progressed upon it, and before I knew it, there were concerts and balls all over Cornwall – from Lanson to 'Zance – featuring me, Josh Emidy! Soon, the money came in. Soon I found myself lead violinist in the Truro Philharmonic Society. I took lodgings – just off Lemon Street – so I could be at the Assembly Rooms quickly. What shenanigans now, eh?

CHORUS*: [*with a flourish*] Ladies and gentlemen of the Duchy of Cornwall, the Truro Philharmonic Society presents the virtuoso violinist Josh Emidy Esquire.

JOSH *enters and bows before the* CHORUS *and audience. The* CHORUS *clap politely.* JOSH *begins to play a piece of chamber music. Here, the* CHORUS *are no longer working-class jowster women, but instead transform into the female socialites of early nineteenth-century Cornish society. The contrast in language is as complete as possible.*

CHORUS*: I say gaals, that fellow Emidy is most agreeable.

CHORUS*: Indeed. He demonstrates just what improvement can do for one.

CHORUS*: I find music such a pleasurable diversion.

CHORUS*: Very true. Very true. I must say though, there seems a plentiful lack of marriageable young men here tonight. Ladies, we shall have to dance unaccompanied.

CHORUS*: My dearest Emelia, now where did you learn such fine locution?

CHORUS*: A new book: 'The Excellency of the English Tongue' by Edward Pellew...

The CHORUS *form dancing sets, creating figures of eights, pousettes, honours and passes typical of the period.* JOSH *continues playing, somewhat embarrassed at all the female attention he is gaining. The* CHORUS *moves toward him and freezes.*

JOSH: [*to the audience*] So this is my world now... How things have changed again! Not the world I had in Lisbon, but just as good. These are the rich daughters of Cornwall's mine owners; the men who made their fortunes out of tin and copper, and now they spend their riches on coming-out gowns, soirees and balls. These leaders of industry spend their time dallying between drawing rooms and coinage halls, worrying over gunnies and granite by day, and gout and gumption by night. And all the while, these young frittering things dream to escape from Cornwall's mist and murk. [*Pause*] I know how they feel. I should be happy. But I cannot be. No artist can ever be happy, for if they are truly an artist, then they are always anxious for the next idea, the one that will be their legacy; the one that will be talked about in a hundred years.

JOSH *starts playing again, and then finishes the song.*

CHORUS*: [*clapping*] Bravo! Bravo!

JOSH: Thank you. Thank you. You ladies are so kind...

The CHORUS *giggles, then exits.* JOSH *strips out of this performance clothing, and moves to a writing position for composing music.*

JOSH: So I find myself like these young women, wanting more, and not finding it. There is a longing in me. An ache. The only way to ease this ache is to compose. I do this early each morning before my teaching begins. What am I writing? Ha – music. Yes. But not just the usual drudge-works I write for the Philharmonic Societies. No. I seek something more. I am writing an opera, the like of which the world has never seen. [*Sighs*] When I write I think back to the birds and insects of Guinea and Brazil. I want to fuse, combine, merge, mix, blend, in ways no one has done before. See this [*holds up the tin violin*]. This helps me. I know it, but I am not sure the world is ready for a Negro composer with an opera in his head.

CHORUS*: [*from off-stage*] Never mind all that boy. When's yer next concert?

JOSH: Next week. [*nervous*]. It's with Signora Griglietti, at the Assembly Rooms. Truro.

CHORUS*: [*off*] Trura, eh? Posh. A bettermost class ov people there. Now, who's she when she's at home?

JOSH: You've not heard of Signora Griglietti? She is the voice of Mozart in Britain. The whole of Cornwall will be there. She has sung upon every stage in the land, and worked with the very best.

CHORUS*: You are the very best. Why dunnee' shaw her what you've written?

JOSH: Griglietti? But...

CHORUS*: But what?

JOSH: You're right. I will show her the music and libretto at this afternoon's rehearsal.

JOSH *clenches his fist and exits, carrying his libretto.*

SIGNORA GRIGLIETTI *enters, wearing stage clothing and carrying a suitcase. She looks somewhat stressed and has obviously been working hard at the rehearsal. A* CHORUS *member fans her.*

CHORUS*: This is your dressing room ma'am... I hope everything is to your satisfaction.

GRIGLIETTI: It will be fine thank you. I simply must practice my scales. My voice is hoarse from the dust of the road. Don't worry... I'll be right as rain for this evening...

CHORUS*: Very well ma'am. I shall leave you now.

GRIGLIETTI *begins to unpack her suitcase. As she does so, she loudly practices her scales.*

GRIGLIETTI: [*tuneless*] Aaaaaaah... Ay-eeeeee... Aaaaawww... Ooooooo. [*more tuneful*] Aaaaaaah... Ay-eeeeee... Aaaaawww... Ooooooo.

Josh enters.

JOSH: Knock. Knock.

GRIGLIETTI *is startled and looks across to* JOSH.

JOSH: The door was open.

GRIGLIETTI: Can I help you?

JOSH: My name is Emidy, ma'am. Josh Emidy. I…

GRIGLIETTI: Of course. You've been accompanying me this afternoon. And doing a fine job, I must say.

JOSH: Thank you, ma'am. I know of all your work. I knew about it in Lisbon. They talked highly of you there…

GRIGLIETTI: You've worked the Teatro do Solitre?

JOSH: I did. In another life. Before here.

GRIGLIETTI: Your violin… I've noticed… It's quite unusual.

JOSH: It's… a… made of tin.

GRIGLIETTI: Of tin. How odd! Wait till I tell them about it in Covent Garden. A blackamoor violinist with a tin instrument. Only in Cornwall, eh?

JOSH: Can I ask? Are you Italian?

GRIGLIETTI: The name?

JOSH: It sounds Italian. You look Italian…

GRIGLIETTI: That's just for show. Of course, I'm not Italian. But in the world of opera, Italy sells, so by degrees, I became Italian. [*Pause*] I was born in Fulham.

Pause.

JOSH: Fulham… That's London, isn't it? How does it feel to play in London?

GRIGLIETTI: The same as anywhere else – only the audience are bigger asses of course!

Pause.

GRIGLIETTI: Is there something you wanted? Really… I must practice.

JOSH: Sorry. Yes. I wondered… I wondered if you would look over this score for me. I wrote it. Maybe this would be something for the London stage? Before you go back, could you look at it? Let me know what you think.

JOSH *hands it to her.*

GRIGLIETTI: I… I'm not sure I…

JOSH: Please.

GRIGLIETTI: Very well. I will cast my eye upon it.

JOSH *moves to the front of the stage.*

GRIGLIETTI *is seen poring over* JOSH*'s libretto, sometimes smiling, sometimes scowling. There is one section that seem to grab her attention more than the rest, and then the rest of the pages are quickly read through, so much so, that she cannot be reading it. At the same time,* JOSH *speaks over her actions. Eventually,* GRIGLIETTI *tosses the libretto to the floor, and she moves to check her hair and dress before leaving her dressing room to perform.*

JOSH: So she agreed to look over it that week, and I have to say, it was a pleasure to accompany her. The Assembly rooms were sold out. She had three standing ovations. She thanked me for my work and I had my own solo spot. We talked of a tour – maybe to the continent. But then she went away…

The CHORUS *enters with* GRIGLIETTI*, seeking her autograph.*

CHORUS*: Sign here Mrs Grigliettyetty, please…

GRIGLIETTI: My pleasure…

CHORUS*: I tell 'ee what – you'm sum singer, maid.

GRIGLIETTI: Why, thank you…

JOSH *pushes through the* CHORUS *towards her.*

JOSH: Signora…? Signora…

GRIGLIETTI: Oh – Mr Emidy. Yes…

JOSH: My opera. Did you read it?

GRIGLIETTI: Yes…

An awkward pause.

JOSH: And...?

GRIGLIETTI: Really, Mr Emidy, you are of some talent... Magical talent even... and clearly a virtuoso, but this, I don't really think it suitable... for the London stage... I'm sorry. It's not the sort of thing they want... It's too much of a mixture...

GRIGLIETTI *hands him back the libretto. The enthusiastic* CHORUS *pushes towards her and she is swamped by them. They push her off stage.*

JOSH *is left alone. He lets the libretto fall to the floor and exits. The* CHORUS *chants sarcastically as the lights dim.*

CHORUS: Crowder... crowder... crowder...
Dean due... Dean due... Dean due...
Groudel... groudel... groudel...
Gweadar... gweadar... gweadar...
Haze gwaze... Haze gwaze... Haze gwaze...

3. A Chapel Anniversary

Lights up. JAMES SILK BUCKINGHAM *and a dejected-looking* JOSH *enter.* JAMES *puts his right arm over* JOSH*'s shoulder.*

JAMES: So tell me, what did she say? In the letter, I mean?

JOSH: Here... Read it for yourself.

JOSH *hands him the letter.*

JAMES: [*reading*] "You see, your colour would be so much against you, that there would be great risk of failure; and it would be a pity to take you from a sphere in which you are now making a handsome livelihood and enjoy a high reputation, on the risk of so uncertain a speculation."

JOSH: See?

JAMES: I see. Tell me again, what exactly is your opera about?

JOSH: It is about here, and it is about my home. About Africa and Cornwall... It has the music of both.

JAMES: I don't think anyone's attempted that kind of thing before.

JOSH: All the more reason to do it then...

JAMES: Perhaps it's a bit ambitious maybe; a bit too modern...

JOSH: I know the quality...

JAMES *sighs, knowing all too well the reasons it will be rejected. Animated, he tries a new tact.*

JAMES: Listen, Josh. It's Falmouth Chapel's anniversary today. Come with me. Put in a guest appearance. They'll love it. You're a hero amongst them...

JOSH: I don't think that is me any more. Besides, I need to go home, to compose... to write...

JAMES: Come, come. You know the Methodists' stance on slavery. What was it Wesley said? He called it 'execrable villainy' and a 'scandal of religion and human nature'. Listen, they don't judge; not like this Griglietti woman. No more composing. [*joking*] All work makes Josh a dull boy!

JOSH: Will there be tea?

JAMES: 'Course there will. Methodists always have tea.

JOSH: No sugar, though?

JAMES: No sugar. Promise. Methodists don't support slaving.

JAMES *and* JOSH *exit.*

The CHORUS *enters with* JANE HUTCHINS. *Chapel organ music initially, but then this fades as the* CHORUS *speaks.*

CHORUS*: Right me lovers...Let's get outside the chapel and onto the preaching pit. You've had your anniversary tea and bun. All ready are 'ee, fur the snail creep?

CHORUS*: We'm ready.

JANE: [*excitedly*] Ready.

CHORUS*: Then strike up the music.

Processional Cornish music begins. The CHORUS *begins to weave the snail creep dance around the stage. The dance is an adaptation of circle dancing where the dancers link fingers and wind into a spiral looking like the shell of a snail. This dance is popular in Brittany and Cornwall, but was integrated into Methodist culture.* JANE *is the final dancer.*

JAMES *and* JOSH *enter.*

JAMES: Go on… Join on the end.

JOSH *joins the snail creep, holding* JANE*'s hand. She smiles at him.*

JAMES *claps.*

The snail creep weaves in and out of itself. The CHORUS *cheer.*

JOSH *and* JANE *find themselves tangled in the mass of bodies, accidentally facing each other.*

JANE: It's Mr Emidy, isn't it?

JOSH: Yes, ma'am. I am Josh Emidy.

JANE: Pleased to meet you, Josh Emidy. I am much enamoured of your music. I heard you play at the Assembly rooms… on your tin violin.

Their conversation is broken by the CHORUS.

CHORUS*: Let's do it again!

JANE *and* JOSH *break from the others. The snail creep starts again, and this time,* JAMES *is pulled in.*

JANE: That was fun wasn't it?

JOSH: I never did this snail creep before…

JANE: I'm out of breath.

JOSH: See James over there… He'll collapse if he's not careful…

JAMES *is being dragged around the snail creep. He already looks exhausted.*

JANE: Shall we walk?

JOSH: If you wish.

JOSH *and* JANE *move away from the dancing, which winds its way off stage.*

JANE: I like your musical compositions, Mr Emidy.

JOSH: You do?

JANE: Better than those hymns we sing…

JOSH: I suppose so.

JANE: They have passion. From Africa I think.

JOSH: Perhaps. I find that most people are not ready for such music.

JANE: Not ready?

JOSH: I am trying to blend my homeland and here.

JANE: You already have, I think.

Pause. They laugh nervously.

JANE: We should go back.

JOSH: I know... Will you be here next week? At chapel, I mean?

JANE: Of course. My father is a lay preacher.

JOSH: Then perhaps you would walk with me? After the service I mean, and with your father's permission. Would he allow someone like me to even talk to you?

JANE: Do not worry, Mr Emidy. My father is a precision Methodist. He will not let the colour of your skin, nor your past, inform his judgment. He judges on deeds and character, not tittle-tattle.

JOSH: That gladdens my heart.

JANE: And mine too.

JOSH: Then I shall see you next Sunday?

JANE: Of course.

As they are speaking JANE's *father,* ZACHARY HUTCHINS, *enters.* JOSH *is about to leave but is greeted by him.*

ZACHARY: Mr Emidy... We have not had the pleasure. So you're the... everyone is speaking about... from... well... you know. [*Pause*] Jane, shall we? If we don't get back any sooner the saffron buns in the oven will be blacker than hell itself...Oh... pardon me... I didn't mean ... When I say black I meant...

JANE: This is my father Josh.

JOSH: A pleasure to meet you Reverend Hutchins. Your sermon today preached much tolerance. Your words meant so much to me.

ZACHARY: Well, the Bible is completely clear.

JOSH: [*smiling*] Yes – completely clear... [*knowingly*] It's there in black... and white yes?

ZACHARY: Quite.

JOSH: I should be going now. Jane… I look forward to seeing you next Sunday. Goodbye Reverend Hutchins. Enjoy your saffron buns.

JOSH *puts out his hand in order to shake* ZACHARY'*s hand. Awkwardly* ZACHARY *shakes it.* ZACHARY *releases it quickly but then* JOSH *unexpectedly hugs him.* ZACHARY *looks shocked but puts his arms around him nevertheless.*

ZACHARY: I see you've gotten rather friendly with that Emidy fellow…

JANE: Josh you mean?

ZACHARY: Yes… Josh… I didn't realise when you were telling me about him that he was…

JANE: Black?

ZACHARY: Um… yes. Well, there are shades of negrescence you know... and he is rather at the 'black end'… of black…

JANE: The 'black end'… of black?

ZACHARY: I'm only thinking of… you…

JANE: What do you mean?

ZACHARY: Well, if you were to start courting… He has it in his eye. I can tell…

JANE: What?

ZACHARY: If it came to marriage. To your nuptials… then children might follow…

JANE: Naturally. And what of it?

ZACHARY: Then… they'd be… you know… not pure…

JANE: Not pure. Whatever do you mean?

ZACHARY: It's not me Jane. It's just what polite society would say. [*whispering*] They'd call them half-caste…

JANE: Half-caste?

ZACHARY: Yes. I believe it's the term used. The sailors speak of it down the docks. They talk of the mulatto girls.

JANE: Well, I don't care... They won't be half anything. They'd be me and Josh together. They'd be fully cast and we'd love them without bounds.

ZACHARY: But you'll be looked upon in certain ways... judged... excluded... Barriers will go up.

JANE: I don't care. You're supposed to be a Methodist. You shouldn't judge a book by its cover. It's what you preach. Besides, you know how well-respected he is in Cornwall.

ZACHARY: Look my darling, take no notice. I'll back you whatever you decide. I just don't want your reputation to be ruined.

JANE: Don't worry about my reputation. I can take care of myself father.

ZACHARY: Come. The buns will be ruined... but we've still got some taa and hevva cake left.

He goes to leave. JANE *halts him from going.*

JANE: I'm going to be with Josh whatever you think. With him I know I'll never be second fiddle.

JOSH *comes back and* JANE *kisses him on the lips.*

JOSH: So we marry, Jane and I, on the 16th of September 1802, and there are children. I name them for you: Joseph, Thomas Hutchins, James, Cecilia, Benjamin and Richard. See how my branches spread now. They become my joy and hope, and though there is no slavery now, I still wonder how will the world judge them? I teach them. I give them my love. Gradually though, I play the tin violin less and less. Its surface becomes dustier, less shiny. Maybe it returns to the hard granite ground whence it came. There are days when the children are gone, when we walk together in the gardens and I don't play. These long fingered hands have grown old, rheumatic and gnarled. The world changes again, jowsters...

CHORUS: You and we both knaw it, Josh Emidy. We've been slowering up too.

JOSH: So some of my music is played, but the pieces I want played, the operas, the concertos, the chamber music, well, they sit in the drawers of my desk unheard. Music must be played. Do you know? I am haunted by Griglietti and her words. [*Pause*] And then when illness comes, I see them all: Eduardo, Queen Maria, Commander Pellew, Jabez, and my good friend Buckingham.

CHORUS: We see 'um too Josh, across the oceans, across time.

JOSH: For one last time, I take out the violin to play it, and then that day, I see death's face in the tin's reflection.

Lights down. Music: A lament, played upon a violin.

4. The Aftermath

JAMES *enters, followed by the* CHORUS.

CHORUS: They Josh's things be 'um?

JAMES: Yes. I'm sorting a few things out for Jane. She asked me to do it, while she prepares the funeral at Kenwyn.

CHORUS: What become ov 'un sir?

JAMES: He passed on in his sleep. In his will, he left me his manuscripts.

CHORUS: You got the music then? Beauty! Now we'n see the mix he dreamed of. I been lookin' forward t'thaa'. We wun't have t'gather up no fragments.

JAMES: No.

CHORUS: What 'ee mean, no? You said boy Josh left 'ee 'is manuscripts.

JAMES: He did. Sadly, there were strict instructions.

CHORUS: Instructions? I dun't like the sound of tha'.

JAMES: Nor did I.

CHORUS: What? Did 'ee have t'donate them t'some hoity-toity fag-pot ov a Londoner?

JAMES: Sadly, no.

CHORUS: What 'ee mean?

JAMES: The will was precisely worded: 'My dear friend and former student James Silk Buckingham is to inherit my musical manuscripts, but I fear my music will never be accepted, as long as black and white remain strangers to each other. Therefore, I must entreat him as my faithful friend to burn them as soon as they reach his possession...'

CHORUS: Thaas' a bugger!

JAMES: His music – his music played on the tin violin – fused his two worlds, the old and the new. Jowster women, I fear it was a bold move; maybe too bold... The world wasn't ready for Emidy.

CHORUS: Then thaas' a proper tragedy.

JAMES: Agreed.

CHORUS: Didn' 'ee think about sneakun' 'um off somewhere, hidin' them up Temple Moors, perhaps?

JAMES: I couldn't. The solicitor insisted. He watched me light the brazier. They slipped through my fingers into the hungry flames.

CHORUS: Shame. S'pause we'd best be goin' home then...

JAMES: Me too. I have to finish my entries on Emidy's life.

The CHORUS *starts to exit. One* CHORUS *member comes back.*

CHORUS: Mr Buckingham, sir?

JAMES: Yes, my good woman...

CHORUS: So what become of that there violin...?

JAMES: You mean the one he composed upon, the tin violin?

CHORUS: 'Es...

JAMES: Do you know, I've no idea? He once told me it was magical.

CHORUS: Aw 'es. We all knew that. Magic finds magic see. It dun't matter where you'm born... It'll seek 'ee out. Anyone from Cornwall d'knaw that...

JAMES: You're right.

CHORUS: Where you off now then, sir?

JAMES: Back to Sheffield... It's been wonderful here. Back down in Flushing again, but parliament'll soon be back to its benches and boring routines... An MP's work is never done.

CHORUS: I'll let 'ee go then sir. Crowder stean. [*softly*] Asalaamaalekum. Naka nga def? Numu demee? Lu bees? [*resigned*] Dara beesul.

JAMES: What did you say? What was that? Was it Cornish?

CHORUS: Nothin'... Just a bit of that there African language Josh learnt me...

JAMES: Truly then, he has made his mark.

CHORUS: I'll be goin' now, sir. [*resigned to her fate*] There be a basket of cod that needs hawkin' round Arwennack Street... 'Twas fresh this morning, you... S'fresh you could still see 'um jumping... like jowsters at a troyl...

All cast except JOSH *on stage. There follows a troyl, which fuses African drumming with Celtic fiddle instrumentation. The* CHORUS *engages with audience to get them dancing and clapping. The dance is celebratory and as wild as possible. When the dance ends, the stage clears and is engulfed in darkness.*

5. Guinea, West Africa

The return to silence is followed by traditional Guinean music, slow and beautiful, played on berimbau. From the darkness a NEW MEMBER OF THE EMID-EE FAMILY *(played by Actor 1) enters, barefooted and wearing only traditional underclothing. A head garment distinguishes him from* JOSH EMIDY. *He is carrying the tin violin like an offering.*

He holds the violin and bow the wrong way round, rubbing the violin across the bow. Realising, he has it the wrong way round, he puts the violin to his chin, and runs the bow across the strings. The tin violin makes a sound. He smiles. The lights dim.

In the darkness, we hear the voice of JABEZ PENDER.

JABEZ: Yeah, yeah. Stupid bugger. Gerrock. Clizzard. Fickia! [*laughs*] Crowder stean... [*slower*] Crowder stean... Dean due. Dean due. Dean due. 'Es, tin violin. [*laughs long and hard*]

– END –

Woods Cafe

Cardinham Woods

Woods Cafe is a beautiful woodsmans cottage set among 600 acres of woodland. we serve home cooked food and local produce.

In our back garden we have a 28ft yurt avaliable for weddings and celebrations, or we can bring our yurt to you.

www.woodscafecornwall.co.uk
woodscafe@live.co.uk
01208 78111

HYUNDAI I20

3 Door or 5 Door Versions
5 Year Unlimited Mileage
Warranty On Every Hyundai

MAKE YOUR OWN
ADVENTURE THIS SUMMER

Hawkins Motors Ltd
Central Garage
Blackwater,
Truro, TR4 8ET
01872 560987

From
£30*
Learn
to
Surf
Qualified Instructors &
Beach Lifeguards
From single* sessions
to full week 'improver' courses
All equipment provided
Family, Group & Student discounts
Guaranteed Fun!
PERRANPORTH SURF SCHOOL
Beach
Lifeguards
SurfingGB
For more information contact us:
Telephone: 07974 550 823
E-mail: info@perranporthsurfschool.co.uk
www.perranporthsurfschool.co.uk

GET CLOSER
Scan to visit our website
CORNWALL'S BIGGEST ZOO
NEWQUAY ZOO
NEW FOR 2012
PAY ONCE & VISIT EVERY DAY FOR A WEEK!
Get closer to over 130 species at award winning Newquay Zoo! Listen to the lions roar, see playful monkeys, slithery snakes and learn more about important conservation in fascinating keeper talks.
An amazing day out for the whole family!
Newquay Zoo, Trenance Gardens, Newquay, Cornwall TR7 2LZ
SAT NAV: TR7 2NN
Tel: (+44) 0844 474 2244
Email: info@newquayzoo.org.uk
NEWQUAY ZOO
WWW.NEWQUAYZOO.ORG.UK

CORNISH
PANTRY
RESTAURANT
At the Cornish Pantry Restaurant we offer you an incredible opportunity to try original meals taken from authentic Cornish recipes as well as an amazing family menu.
THE ORIGINAL
MINERS
PASTY
PLATTER
NEWLYN
FISH
PLATTER
Treasure Park, Tolgus Mill
Nr Redruth, Cornwall TR16 4HN
01209 203 289 www.treasureparks.com

VISIT SKINNERS BREWERY IN TRURO

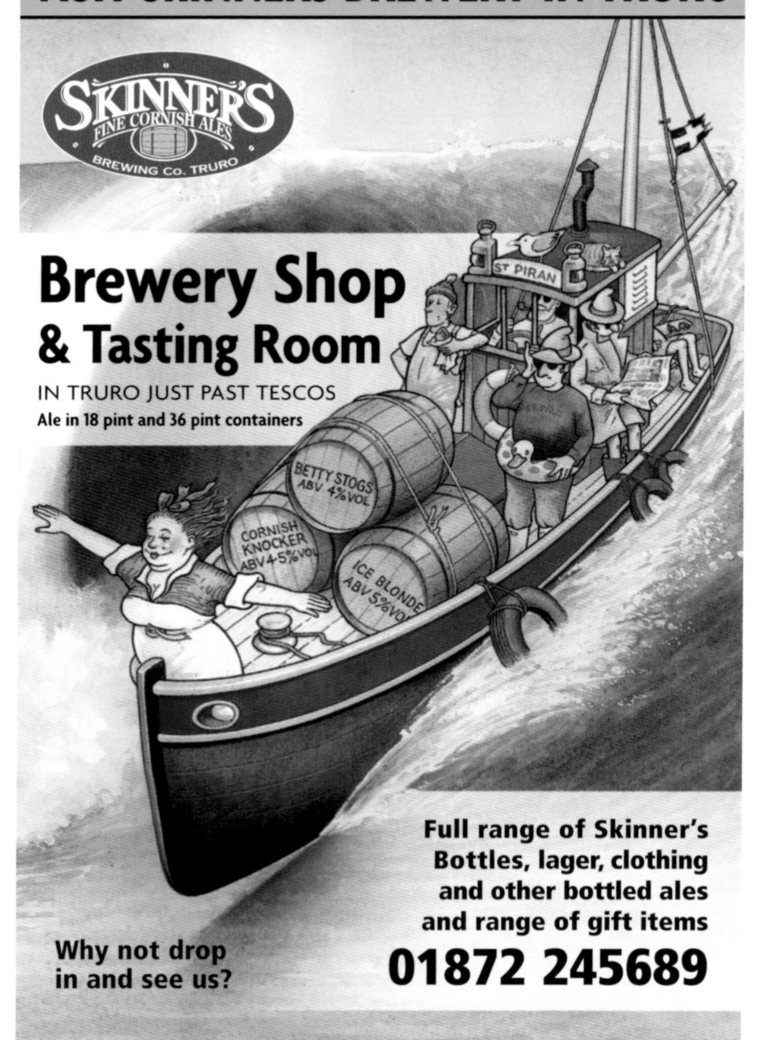

VISITOR CENTRE OPEN DAILY FOR TOURS & TASTINGS

LOENTER
Mawnan Smith - Falmouth
10% discount* on all weekly rates if you mention Bish Bash Bosh !
The ideal spot to relax at anytime of the year
Spacious s/c holiday accommodation sleeps up to 3.
In ground floor annexe of detached house in 2 acres of land in the delightful village of Mawnan Smith. Close to beautiful Helford River and within walking distance of a number of acclaimed gardens. Free wi-fi, plenty of parking and secure storage for bicycles.
To book or for more info please email loenter@hotmail.com
or phone 01326 250 403